D1634057

Svedenstierna's Tour

SVEDENSTIERNA'S TOUR GREAT BRITAIN 1802-3

The Travel Diary of an Industrial Spy

Eric T. Svedenstierna

TRANSLATED FROM THE GERMAN BY
E. L. DELLOW
WITH A NEW INTRODUCTION BY
M. W. FLINN
PROFESSOR OF SOCIAL HISTORY IN
THE UNIVERSITY OF EDINBURGH

DAVID & CHARLES
Newton Abbot

0 7153 5747 6

*Set in eleven point Linotype Baskerville
two points leaded
and printed in Great Britain
by W J Holman Limited Dawlish
for David & Charles (Holdings) Limited
South Devon House Newton Abbot
Devon*

Contents

Introduction
to the English Edition

In an age of scientific and trade journals, of patent specification lists and international technical aid, it is hard to appreciate that one of the most acute problems facing industrialists of former centuries was that of keeping abreast with technological advance. Even within a single industry of one country, and without the aid of patent protection, it was possible, in the eighteenth century, say, for the discoverer of a new manufacturing technique to keep his secret and its advantages to himself for many years, even decades, before it might become generally available to his competitors. Internationally, the barriers to the diffusion of new technologies were even greater, sometimes to the point of being all but insuperable. Industrial spying was a common method of tackling the problem, and the migration of skilled workers, sometimes lured by high rewards, another method commonly practised. Some of the newer techniques of Britain's industrial revolution were widely diffused through Europe by skilled British workers.[1]

The exchange, however, worked both ways, and so long as Sweden retained the leadership of European iron manufacture, ironmasters themselves made visits there to find out about the latest technological developments. Sir Ambrose Crowley, for example, the great iron manufacturer of the North of England of the late seventeenth and early eighteenth centuries, sent his younger half-brother, Benjamin, to Sweden in 1701 with a detailed schedule of queries concerning iron manufacture which he was to investigate in the course of a visit of nearly twelve months.[2] The visit of the son of Samuel Garbett, the Birmingham industrialist, to Sweden for similar purposes in 1763 is better known. Garbett claimed that his son made 'important discoveries' during the visit 'which have already been put into practice, and will prove a national advantage'.[3]

As Britain gradually assumed the technological leadership of Europe in her industrial revolution, it is not surprising that the flow of technological visits turned more and more towards her. Britain became something of a Mecca for the technicians of other European countries towards the end of the eighteenth century. Some of the foreigners who came to study British techniques are well known. One of the earliest such visitors, of course, was Peter the Great, but on the level of practical technicians, the Frenchman Gabriel Jars in 1764[4] and Marchant de la Houlière in 1794[5] are perhaps best known. From Germany, Caspar Voght came in 1793 to study primarily British agricultural methods during a two-year visit,[6] while Johann Conrad Fischer made two journeys to Britain from Switzerland in 1794 and 1814 for the purpose of studying current methods in the metallurgical industries.[7]

In the late eighteenth century, it was, above all, Sweden that had best cause for showing an awareness of technological advances in Britain. Until well into the middle of the eighteenth century the Swedish iron industry had predominated in the European market. Though the British industry was far from insignificant in the early eighteenth century, and had been responding positively to a steadily growing demand in both home and colonial markets,[8] imports of Swedish iron had grown remorselessly from the late seventeenth century to bridge the gap between British requirements and home supplies. By the mid-eighteenth century, possibly half the iron consumed in Britain was imported, three-quarters of it coming from Sweden. Britain's dependence upon Sweden, reinforced by further vital imports of timber and other 'naval stores', was matched reciprocally by Sweden's dependence on the British market: in the middle of the eighteenth century, bar iron comprised about 60 per cent of Sweden's total exports, and of this, 55 per cent was normally sent to Britain. From the middle of the century, however, Russian exports began to compete effectively with Swedish bar iron in the British market, and by the 1770s British imports of Russian iron actually overtook imports from Sweden. This diminution of Sweden's share of the British trade was, however, relative, not absolute. Swedish exports to Britain, running at about 15-20,000 tons per year, maintained this level through the second half of the eighteenth century, in spite of the rise of Russian competition and the more ominous development of the British industry itself.[9] It was able to do this largely on account of the special quality of Swedish irons: for certain purposes, particularly steelmaking, Swedish bar iron remained indispensable.

As the eighteenth century drew to its close, however, for Swedish ironmasters the writing was on the wall. If, on account of the remoteness of the Urals and inability to develop beyond a certain, very limited point, the Russian iron industry never really drove home its threat to Sweden, the dangers from the developments in Britain were much more apparent. Swedish ironmasters became increasingly conscious that, at any moment, technological advances in British iron-and-steel making might render Swedish imports superfluous. The whole foundation of the Swedish industrial economy seemed in danger of being undermined by the potentialities of new technologies.

The development of the British iron industry in the second half of the eighteenth century was based on two main technological advances: coke-smelting and the puddling process. From the first of these, the Swedes had relatively little to fear. Their access to virtually inexhaustible supplies of charcoal kept them clear of the threat of dwindling fuel supply and rising marginal costs that were leading British ironmasters to turn to coke-smelting. For many purposes, too, charcoal iron was purer and more trouble-free than coke iron. Puddling, on the other hand, really did constitute a threat to the Swedish industry. Probably 90 per cent of the total demand for iron in the late eighteenth century was for bar rather than cast iron, and forging, the usual method of converting pig iron from the blast furnace into bar iron, was a slow and expensive process. Cort's inventions of puddling and rolling in 1783 and 1784 were important because they broke through this bottleneck, freeing the British forgemaster at one stroke from the twin tyrannies of labour-intensiveness and dependence on charcoal supplies. For puddling was cheaper than forging in terms both of fuel and labour costs. With unlimited access to coal, British ironmasters gained overnight an advantage over their Swedish competitors to whom, without coal, the lower costs of puddling were inaccessible. Like so many other important inventions in its early stages, however, puddling was initially imperfect and not immediately taken up by all ironmasters. But the threat to Sweden of the ultimate perfection of the process and its general adoption by the British industry was clear enough to the Swedish ironmasters.

Seen from across the North Sea, therefore, the technical advances of the late eighteenth century in British ironmaking carried the very real threat of the extinction of Sweden's principal manufacturing industry.[10] It was a threat of which the Swedes had been conscious long before Cort's discoveries. They had, in fact, been keeping the British industry under close surveillance throughout the eighteenth century. A long succession of well-qualified technicians had toured Britain at frequent intervals, studying current methods of production and reporting back to Sweden in a series of travel-diaries and reports which today constitutes an invaluable if still little-used source of information about British industry of the eighteenth century.[11] It was possible for the Swedish iron industry to maintain this systematic and sustained watch on the progress of British iron technology in the eighteenth century because it was highly and efficiently organised. Not only had there been since the early seventeenth century a separate government department specifically devoted to the interests of the industry, the Board of Mining and Metallurgical Industries (Bergs-Kollegium), which itself had been responsible for sending technical experts to study British conditions,[12] but from the mid-eighteenth century the ironmasters themselves formed an institution which was to make a very positive contribution to both the organisation and the technical efficiency of the industry. The Jernkontor, or Iron Bureau, was created in 1747 by the Bruks Societet, or Association of Ironmasters.[13] Its purpose was to find collective solutions to the problems of production, organisation, finance, and technology which had dogged the Swedish industry during the previous twenty years. The Jernkontor was effectively the executive body of the Ironmasters' Association and was manned by a permanent staff of financial and technical experts. Some of the leading authorities on iron and steel technology in the late eighteenth century, like Sven Rinman, were permanent employees of the Jernkontor. The Jernkontor quickly established a very real control over the operation of iron-making by the appointment from the 1750s of övermasmästere, or technical superintendents. The appointment of Rinman, already with valuable experience in the service of the Bergs-Kollegium behind him, to the first of such posts with responsibility for an important geographical area of ironmaking quickly yielded significant dividends in terms of costs and quality.

One of Rinman's assistants, Bengt Quist Anderson, was amongst those sent to Britain in 1766-7 to study the state of technology in the British iron industry. He made a particular study of the new cast-steel process.[14]

In the crisis of the turn of the nineteenth century, when the interruptions of trade due to war added to the disadvantages Sweden was beginning to feel from the emergence of puddling in Britain, it was on the *Jernkontor* that the responsibility for action fell. At this time, one of the leading officials of the *Jernkontor* was Eric Thomas Svedenstierna. Svedenstierna was one of the new school of Swedish metallurgists who were seeking a better understanding of metallurgical processes through a knowledge of theoretical chemistry. The identification of oxygen in the 1770s and the recognition that it was the carbon content that largely differentiated pig iron, wrought iron and steel from each other opened up important new possibilities in the study of metallurgy.

Advances both in theoretical metallurgy and practical technology, therefore, underlay the *Jernkontor's* concern with the long-run prospects of the Swedish industry. To the more perceptive economists and ironmasters in Sweden it was apparent that the only hope for their industry's survival in the new conditions of the nineteenth century would be to concentrate on high quality products. But shifts of this kind within the whole industry were not to be accomplished overnight, and in the meantime the French wars, with their major disruptions to the normal courses of European commerce, endangered the short-run position and robbed the industry of the time necessary to adjust to the changing technological environment. In response to the needs of war finance, the British started to raise their import duties on Swedish iron from 1796. Exports to Britain had fallen in the short run from around 25,000 tons in 1793 to a mere 15,000 tons in 1798. The French and

Mediterranean markets, which had grown to some significance in the last third of the eighteenth century, also slumped disastrously during the 1790s.[15] The development of the American market, which was to play a valuable part in sustaining the output of the industry during the first half of the nineteenth century, was slow and of no real importance before 1810.[16]

These, then, were the dire circumstances in which Svedenstierna was dispatched by the *Jernkontor* in 1810 to tour France and Britain in search of scientific knowledge, mainly chemistry, which could assist the re-orientation of the Swedish industry. Unfortunately, very little is known of Svedenstierna's life. Born in 1765, he seems to have been in the service of the *Jernkontor* by 1796, where he subsequently became director of pig iron production. He has left no account of his tour in France, but wrote a detailed account of his visit to Britain during the winter and early spring of 1802/3. Back at the *Jernkontor* he became the first editor of *Jernkontorets Annaler*. This periodical, devoted to the discussion of technical and economic aspects of ironmaking, first appeared in 1817 and has continued publication ever since. Svedenstierna also published a number of shorter articles, mainly about steelmaking methods in Sweden and elsewhere, between 1805 and 1811.[17] Earlier he had translated French writings on iron and steel metallurgy into Swedish.[18] He died in 1825.

'The intention of my journey to England', he wrote at the beginning of his Tour,[19] 'was actually to get to know methods of ironmaking there'. It was not easy, however, for a foreigner to do this. It was, firstly, very difficult to find out before setting off which were the major ironworks, and where they were. 'Neither natives, who dealt in iron, nor proprietors of ironworks, of whom I had already got to know several, could indicate to me exactly what route I would have to take in order to see the most and the largest ironworks, what difficulty a foreigner would encounter in his inquiries, etc.'[20] This difficulty was finally overcome by the assiduous study of guide-books and the systematic use of letters of introduction from the Swedish Consul-General in London and several of the distinguished scientists he met in London before setting out for the provinces. The second problem concerned the ethics of industrial spying. Svedenstierna was, after all, under instruction from the *Jernkontor* to find out all he could about British manufacturing methods. There were many instances in history —Huntsman and his crucible steelmaking process, for example—of operators of new processes being extremely secretive and unwilling to allow visitors to see the inside of their works, not least when these were overseas competitors. Svedenstierna knew well enough that successful industrial spying often involved desperate subterfuges of doubtful morality. He turned his face against such methods, however, determining to 'go no further in the matter than the rules of hospitality allowed'.[21] Instead he relied on introductions from men of sufficient status and authority to raise him above suspicion.

He also took an opportunity that was presented to him to travel in company. Arriving at Dover alone, he travelled first to London, and it was only there that Mr Charles Greville, of interest to Svedenstierna on account of his valuable collection of minerals, suggested to him that he might travel in the company of a French engineer, August Henri de Bonnard, no doubt taking advantage of the interruption to hostilities between France and Britain brought about by the Peace of Amiens to examine recent developments in British industry. De Bonnard was a younger man than Svedenstierna, having been born probably about 1780. He graduated from the Ecole Polytechnique in 1799 and was appointed *ingénieur des mines* in 1801. By 1811 he was Secretary of the *Conseil Général des Mines*, a government department of which he also, in 1824, became divisional inspector. In addition to his tour of Britain with Svedenstierna in 1802-3, he had spent several years in Germany. From 1803 publications flowed freely from his pen, starting with a group of articles deriving from information gleaned on his visit to Britain. Like Svedenstierna, he was particularly interested in the latest techniques of iron manufacture.[22]

After a stay of two months in London during which he visited all the principal scientific institutions, established acquaintance with influential people whose letters of introduction were to be the means of gaining access to industrial sites up and down the country, learning about coaching, inns, and travel in Britain generally, and, lastly, making the acquaintance of his travelling companion, August Henri de Bonnard, Svedenstierna finally set out on his industrial tour in March 1803. Because of de Bonnard's main interest in mines, Svedenstierna was obliged to delay getting to grips with the iron industry, and the pair of foreign travellers visited first south-west England. Not until they had crossed the Bristol Channel by boat from Ilfracombe to Swansea was Svedenstierna at last able to begin his study of British ironmaking methods. He obviously enjoyed himself greatly in South Wales, visiting the famous ironworks at Plymouth, Cyfarthfa, Pen-y-daren, Dowlais, Sirhowy, and Tredegar. Like Manchester to a textile expert, this ironmaking area of South Wales in the first years of the nineteenth century symbolised to a metallurgist the Industrial Revolution. What so impressed the visitor from Sweden was the scale of everything he saw—the number of works, the magnitude of the output, and the sheer size of the plant and machines. His excitement at his first glimpse of the new industrial age is undisguised and he left South Wales with obvious reluctance. His companion, de Bonnard, however, was anxious to press on, and they made their way quickly northwards to the industrial Midlands where their first visit was the essential pilgrimage for all iron men—to the very birthplace of the Industrial Revolution at Coalbrookdale. At Birmingham, de Bonnard left him to return to France, and Svedenstierna continued his journey alone.[23] From the Midlands, choosing a 'metallurgical' route with a connoisseur's perception through Sheffield and Rotherham, he made his way to the North-East. Using Newcastle as a base he visited many industrial sites on Tyneside before pushing on to Scotland. Here he moved about busily, missing very little that was important to his purpose. Finally, after about eight weeks of incessant travelling and sight-seeing, he turned south, taking the west coast route in order to pass through Lancashire on his return journey.

When, in mid-May 1803, war with France was renewed, Svedenstierna, still progressing leisurely and purposefully in the North of England, decided to abandon the rest of his tour and return home. The hazards of travel as a foreigner, the suspicions aroused, and the resultant inconveniences would be too great. Svedenstierna therefore made tracks by the quickest route to London where war shipping difficulties caused a delay of several weeks before he was finally able to take ship for Sweden.

Though a desire to visit ironworks dictated his choice of route, Svedenstierna retained throughout his tour his catholicity of interest, and took in visits to any kind of industrial undertaking to which he could get access. He was particularly interested in some of the recent developments in industrial transport and commented fully on many of the canals and tramways he saw. Novelties, like inclined planes, fascinated him, and he had a keen eye for the engineering problems of mines. Above all, however, he showed great shrewdness of economic observation. What concerned him was not so much the novelty of the processes he inspected as their economic viability. He penetrated, in other words, to the core of technological progress in noticing that the new processes were important because they lowered unit costs. When discussing, for example, the manufacture of iron and steel spades at the Cramond works outside Edinburgh, he noted that it was the size of the market which, by permitting large-scale production, made it possible to produce these articles more cheaply than they could have been made in Sweden.[24] He also observed that the cause of David Mushet's business failure was his inability to take adequate account of economic realities.[25] At a different level, but with equal perception, he pointed out that the importance of the Duke of Bridgewater's Worsley canal lay in 'its decisive influence on imitators'.[26] The *Jernkontor* had clearly selected a representative who combined an expert's understanding with both tact and economic shrewdness.

While waiting in London he decided that what he had seen during his tour was sufficiently interesting to be worth writing out in a book. The result was the first Swedish edition of the *Tour*, published in 1804.[27] In 1811, Johann Blumhof produced a German translation of the Swedish original,[28] and it is from this German version that the present, the first, English version has now been prepared. For reasons not explained by the German translator, the last two pages of the original Swedish version were not translated and did not appear in the German edition. They have now been translated from the Swedish original and appear in the present edition. Blumhof, himself a metallurgist in state employment, embellished the German edition with some quite comprehensive footnotes. These have been retained in the present edition where, so far as possible, they have been corrected and presented according to modern bibliographical conventions. In the text itself the present editor has added a few bibliographical com-

xvii

ments and corrections of personal and place names. These have been inserted in square brackets.

The *Tour* does not set out to be a scientific work. It was obviously written with a fairly general readership in mind. Nonetheless, Svedenstierna had acquired a great deal of technical and economic information about British iron-making in the course of his visit. His German translator, Blumhof, in his preface, expressed the hope that Svedenstierna would soon give to the world 'the metallurgical observations which he made on this interesting tour'.[29] This he did in 1813 in a scholarly and substantial work with historical, economic, and scientific sections which still awaits a translator and a modern edition.[30]

1 Examples of the work of many of these British technicians abroad are given by W. O. Henderson in *Britain and Industrial Europe, 1750-1870* (Liverpool, 1954).
2 Directions given to Mr Benjamin Crowley, 3 November 1701. MS. in possession of Mr Humphrey Lloyd, Wotton-under-Edge, Glos, to whom I am indebted for access.
3 *Calendar of Home Office Papers*, 1760-1765, No. 1359.
4 Gabriel Jars, *Voyages Métallurgiques* (3 vols, Lyon and Paris, 1774-81). See also J. Chevalier, 'La mission de Gabriel Jars dans les mines et les usines Britanniques en 1764', *Transactions of the Newcomen Society*, XXVI (1947-9).
5 W. H. Chaloner, 'Marchant de la Houlière's Report to the French Government on British Methods of Smelting Iron Ore with Coke. . . , *Edgar Allen News*, Dec. 1948 and Jan. 1949.
6 Gerhard Ahrens, *Caspar Voght und sein Mustergut Flottbek* (Hamburg, 1969).
7 K. Schib and R. Gnade, *Johann Conrad Fischer, 1773-1854* (Schaffhausen, 1954). For further examples of foreign study of British technological progress during the Industrial Revolution, see H. J. Teuteberg, 'Der Ausbau der Englischen Binnen- und Kütenschiffahrt während der Frühindustrialisierung im Spiegel zeitgenössischer deutscher Reiseberichte'; and the same author's 'Die Industrialisierung der britischen Seeschiffahrt in deutschen Augenzeugenberichten zwischen 1750 und 1850', both in *Technik Geschichte*, XXXIV (1967).
8 M. W. Flinn, 'The growth of the English iron industry, 1660-1760', *Economic History Review*, 2nd ser. XI (1958-9).
9 K.-G. Hildebrand, 'Foreign markets for Swedish iron in the 18th century', *Scandinavian Economic History Review*, VI (1958).
10 E. Söderlund, 'The impact of the British Industrial Revolution on the

Swedish iron industry', in L. S. Pressnell (ed.), *Studies in the Industrial Revolution* (1960).

11 See M. W. Flinn, 'The travel-diaries of Swedish engineers of the eighteenth century as sources of technological history', *Transactions of the Newcomen Society*, XXXI (1957-8 and 1958-9). Though the focus of the travel-diarists was primarily on iron manufacture, they showed a wide cultural range. Many visitors came from Sweden unconnected with iron manufacture and with broader scientific interests. (See S. Rydberg, *Svenska Studieresor till England under Frihetstiden* (Uppsala, 1951).

12 Samuel Schröderstierna, for example, who was employed by the *Bergskollegium* from 1738 to 1771, was sent to Britain between 1748 and 1751. (See M. W. Flinn, 'Samuel Schröderstierna's "Notes on the English iron industry" (1749), translated from the Swedish with notes, *Edgar Allen News* (August, 1954).

13 The history of *Jernkontoret* has been very fully covered by B. Boëthius and A. Kromnow, *Jernkontorets Historia* (3 vols, Stockholm, 1947-50). There is a useful short summary in English by G. Arpi, 'The Swedish Ironmasters' Association', *Scandinavian Economic History Review*, VIII (1960).

14 See B. Q. Anderson, *Anmärkningar samlade på resan i England åren 1766 och 1767.* MS. in Jernkontoret, Stockholm.

15 For a full account of the difficulties of the Swedish iron industry in this period see K.-G. Hildebrand, *Fagerstabrukens Historia: Sexton- och Sjutton-hundratalen* (Uppsala, 1957), pp.360-371.

16 E. W. Fleischer, 'The beginning of the transatlantic market for Swedish iron', *Scandinavian Economic History Review*, I (1953).

17 For a list of these, see C. Sahlin, *Svenkst Stål* (Stockholm, 1931), p.227.

18 E. T. Svedenstierna (trans.), *Herrar Vandermonde's, Bertholetts och Monge's Afhandling om Jernet betraktadt i dess olika Tilstand af Tackjern, smidigt Jern och Stål* (Uppsala, 1796).

19 P8 below.

20 P22 below.

21 P9 below.

22 E. G., A. H. de Bonnard, 'Sur les procédés employés en Angleterre pour le traitement du fer par le moyen de la houille', *Journal des Mines*, XVII (An 13 [1804]). A full bibliography of his publications is given in *Note des Travaux Minéralogiques de M. de Bonnard* (Paris, 1827). I am much indebted to Professor François Crouzet and M. André Thépot for copies of this and other material relating to de Bonnard.

23 The section of Svedenstierna's book dealing with the Midlands was separately translated (also from the German edition) and published by W. A. Smith with useful annotations as 'A Swedish view of the West Midlands in 1802-1803', in *West Midlands Studies*, III (1969), 45-72.

24 P176 below.

25 P198 below.

26 P228 below.

27 Eric Th. Svedenstierna, *Resa Igenom en del af England och Skottland åren 1802 och 1803* (Stockholm, 1804).

28 Johann Georg Ludolph Blumhof (trans), *Erich Th. Svedenstierna's*

Eric Th. Svedenstierna's

TOUR

through a part of
ENGLAND and SCOTLAND
in the years 1802 and 1803
with particular reference
to mining and metallurgical, technological
and mineralogical matters

TRANSLATED FROM THE SWEDISH
WITH SOME OBSERVATIONS AND EXPLANATIONS
BY

JOH. GEORGE LUDOLPH BLUMHOF

D.D.W. DOCTOR, MASTER OF ARTS, GRAND-DUCAL
INSPECTOR OF MINES FOR LUDWIGSHÜTTE
AND MEMBER OF SEVERAL LEARNED SOCIETIES

Marburg and Kassel
Joh. Chr. Krieger
1811

Introduction
to the German Edition

Learned journals have long since made up their minds about the value and contents of the travel book of which I here offer a German translation. The original was published in Stockholm by Carl Deelen in 1804, under the title: *Resa igenom en del af England och Skottland, åren 1802 och 1803; af Eric Th. Svedenstierna,* 329 pages in octavo. The author travelled at the expense of the Swedish Metallurgical Society, and had the opportunity, through his numerous acquaintances and letters of introduction, to see and to learn much which is not possible for an ordinary traveller provided with less valuable references, especially in England. The contents of this little work cannot therefore fail to attract the metallurgical and technological readership, and this also induced me, soon after the appearance of the original, to announce a German translation in the advertising columns of the Halle general Literary Journal. However, the political situation of Sweden prevented me from obtaining the original through my Stockholm friends, until I finally succeeded in doing so through the kind offices of my friend and countryman, General Inspector Hausmann, of Kassel. The latter brought back the work from his mineralogical tour through Sweden and Norway, and was kind enough to lend it to me for translation, for which I here publicly record my gratitude. I am convinced that no one will lay aside this little work without interest, especially since we appear to have lacked, until now, thorough information about the English iron works.

Where Mr S. has, in the interests of brevity, merely touched upon some matters, I have in the notes made reference to publications which give fuller information. It is indeed astonishing to read to what degree of completeness the factory system has attained in England. However, in this connection it should not be forgotten that so many circumstances there concur to make this possible, in which respect rich men of private means, thick coal seams, facilitation of inland trade by accessible canals, as well as the monopoly of sea trade, deserve special attention. Thereby so much is possible in England and Scotland which we in Germany can only admire, but not emulate. However, accounts such as the author gives us serve at any rate to awaken ingenuity, to stimulate emulation, and at least not to leave unused the resources which Nature offers us and a wise legislation protects.

The tin smelting process at Truro in Cornwall has been described and explained by Prof. Lampadius in his *Handbook of general Metallurgy*, part 2 Vol. 3, page 66 et seq (Göttingen, 1809, 8vo). [W. A. Lampadius, *Handbuch der allgemeinen Hüttenkunde* (Göttingen, 1801-10).]

May it soon please Director Svedenstierna to give us the metallurgical observations which he made on this interesting tour.

Ludwigshütte near Biedekopf, in the Grand Duchy of Hessen, March 1810.

J. G. L. Blumhof

Chapter I

London

TOWARDS THE END OF NOVEMBER 1802 I ARRIVED, AFTER A
few days journey from Paris via Calais, in Dover. In Calais
the traveller must show and sign his passport immediately
after arrival, and also have his luggage inspected, the earlier
the better, because he cannot otherwise depart with the first
packet boat, or must at least have his goods taken quickly to
the Customs House and from there back on board, whereby
something is often lost. The export of French gold and
silver coins is forbidden. It is best, therefore, to change such
coins, which one may be carrying, for guineas or banknotes,
to which end one seeks out the landlord or a good business
house, and entrusts them with the transaction, otherwise in
the inns an attempt may be made to cheat the traveller
with debased if not often counterfeit coins.

While the packet boat cruised before the harbour of
Dover, various boats appeared, to take the passengers ashore
for a special fee. This is usually considerable, and one takes
advantage of these offers only under special circumstances.
As soon as the packet boat arrives at the quay at Dover, the
luggage of the passengers is taken to the Customs House,
where the owner must declare, before the inspection, everything which can be dutiable. If this is not done, the duti-
fiable goods are confiscated by the inspector. If, however,
one declares everything all the petty annoyances to which a
traveller is subjected in some other countries are avoided.
As proof of this I must mention that I and three travelling

companions already had our luggage in the hotel where we were staying, half an hour after setting foot on land; a case of instruments, maps and books, for which if they had acted strictly according to law, I should have had to pay at least a third of the value, were charged with a mere half-crown duty, because they were considered necessary for the purpose of my journey. Also in Dover the passport must be shown, and one receives a written permit, which contains a description of the traveller, and is signed by the latter. One must keep this carefully until departure from England, when it will be demanded back by the Aliens Office[1] where the passport is signed upon departure. Should this pass be lost, one must try to procure a new one from the Aliens Office, since no stranger is allowed out of the country until he has shown such a certificate of his arrival.

Dover is in itself not very remarkable, except on account of its chalk cliffs and the fine view of the Channel and the French coast, which latter, however, is only visible in clear weather. Here, as in all other places where the packet vessels land, everything is dearer, and travellers who want to go direct to London do best to depart with the first mail coach or another public vehicle. In such a case it is a matter of indifference at what time of day one approaches the capital. If, however, one travels by one's own coach or by post-chaise, it is safer so to apportion the time that one reaches London in daylight, because one is most exposed to the danger of robbery in the neighbourhood of the town itself. Between Dover and London, nothing appeared which deserved my special attention, except a few small foundries and glass furnaces, besides the shipyard at Chatham and the powder mills at Dartford, which, however, cannot be seen without special permission.

Upon arrival in London, it is best to stay in the inn where the coach stops, until one has decided upon a lodging to one's liking. In this, it is necessary to take the advice of someone who knows the town, for one otherwise runs the risk in the fashionable part sometimes of coming to live in a house of ill-fame or in a street which one may not name without exposing oneself to people's scorn. However, there are in every quarter of the town, and at any time, good rooms to let at all possible prices, according to their situation and character. A traveller, who has business in the neighbourhood of learned institutions, and comes into contact with either scholars or with persons of rank, and must therefore lodge in the western part of London, must reckon upon no less a rent than one and a half to two guineas per week. For this rent one gets merely the room and its cleaning, and is therefore obliged to employ a servant who, if he is to be loyal, also receives one and a half guineas per week. Although it would be possible, even in this part of the town, to live fairly cheaply in certain tiny taverns or eating houses, it is almost a rule for a foreigner who is seeking good acquaintanceship, to visit the better taverns, where, even with all possible economy, one cannot eat for less than five English shillings per day. It is therefore necessary to reckon upon an expenditure of at least five guineas per week merely for rent, service, and food, if one wants to live in this part of the town. On the other hand, in other, more outlying quarters of the town, one can have a respectable room, as well as service and meals, for half as much, perhaps for two guineas a week.

As soon as one is settled in, one must procure a plan of London, partly in order to find one's way about this far-flung and enormous mass of buildings, partly to determine every day the route to be taken to meet those people with whom one has to talk, in the shortest time and with the smallest expenditure on hackney carriages, or indeed to be able to do one's business at all. Besides this plan, a well-printed guidebook is necessary, several different editions and formats of which are encountered in every bookshop.

However, the one which now appears under the title *The picture of London for 1803, being a correct guide to all the curiosities, amusements, etc,* is the most reliable, and is so complete that through a mere reading of it one gets to know London better, and receives more information about the objects which are notable for a traveller, than from persons who have actually lived there for several years.

Travel in whichever land you will, it is always useful to know the whys and wherefores; so that before everything else a travelling plan must be worked out and good letters of introduction and addresses procured. This is essential for anyone who wants to travel to England. There is perhaps no country in the world where a letter of introduction from a known and respected man, be he of high or low rank, learned or unlearned, to his friends, can assure the traveller of a good reception as it can here, where on the other hand ordinary letters of recommendation and introductions mean less. I had been told about this already in Paris by several persons, who had been in England, and on that account I only took a few letters with me to London. I afterwards found that only two of these letters were more than sufficient for my purpose, and I presented the others more out of politeness than on account of the service which they could obtain for me.

It was as little in accordance with the intentions of the Bruk Society [The Swedish Association of Ironmasters—see Introduction, p.xi] as with my own inclination, to travel as a spy, to find out a few tricks of the trade or to wheedle out certain secret manufacturing processes in deceitful fashion; on that account I had already explained to several scholars and friends in France that I merely studied chemistry and mineralogy in order to widen my knowledge in manufacturing methods. The intention of my journey to England was actually to get to know methods of ironmaking there, and the works connected with it; I would, however, go no further in the matter than the rules of hospitality allowed. After such an avowal it was indeed necessary to seek out, immediately upon my arrival in London, the acquaintanceship of knowledgeable and learned people, who could appreciate the actual purpose of my tour, and who could at the same time protect me by their authority against unfounded suspicions. For this purpose, as I have said, only two letters of introduction were necessary. The one from Vauquelin [Louis Nicolas Vauquelin, 1763-1829], who is as greatly esteemed and honoured in England on account of his personal character as he is famous throughout Europe on account of his profound knowledge of chemistry, charmed for me the way to the most distinguished chemists in London. Through the other letter, which was addressed by a French mine superintendent to Count Bournon [Jacques-Louis, Compte de Bournon, 1751-1825], I obtained free entry to several private collections of minerals, whose owners not only showed me much kindness, but some of them rendered me specially important services.

Perhaps it would here be in order to give an exact and exhaustive description of the many good public and private institutions for the propagation of science which London has to show; because, however, some of these institutions are long since well known, and the others do not actually belong here, I will merely try to give a short idea of those which deserve the attention of a travelling miner and metallurgist.

Royal Institution. This institution, which has as its object the general spread of science and its application to arts and handicrafts, was founded about three years ago by the famous Count Rumford. It was designed on a great plan typical of all English undertakings, and the scheme was carried into execution by the usual means of a voluntary subscription. The complete establishment had been estimated to cost £23,000 sterling, and in a short time, not only had this sum been collected by subscription, but certain trustees had offered another £7,000 in case the Institution should need it. The trustees, among whom are some of the highest persons in the state, immediately obtained royal sanction for this Institution, which was thereupon named the Royal Institution. A large house in Albemarle Street was bought for it, which, following the plan, is equipped in the following manner.

On the ground floor there is a carpenter's workshop for the preparation of models, a tinsmith's workshop, another for fine instruments and apparatus, a kitchen for experiments on the preparation of food, in order to make foodstuffs more nourishing and at the same time better tasting, according to the principles of Rumford, particularly for the lower classes, to economise fuel, etc. On the first floor are several reading rooms, in which can be found the best English and foreign journals for all the sciences, with the exception of theology and politics, which, from the scientific point of view, are not considered to be in accordance with the objects of the Institution, and are therefore excluded by its statutes from the reading rooms as well as from the library. In another room there are the leading foreign daily papers, in another, on the other hand, every English newspaper and advertiser. The remaining part of this floor consists of the staircase to the second floor and of a large room, which forms the entrance hall, where a janitor is present all the time, as well as a few smaller rooms for the offices, printing shop, etc.

On the second floor is a hall for chemical lectures and for experimental physics. This has room for 900 to 1,000 persons in comfort, and is in every respect the best and most complete that I have seen, even earlier in Holland and France. The room itself is in the form of a rotunda, into which the light falls from above through a large window. The seats are all of circular formation, and built like an amphitheatre, so that the professor can be seen and heard equally well from all points; the latter has his place and apparatus on the periphery of the outermost circle. In order to prevent crowding upon entry and exit, every row of seats is divided by two gangways, and so that the noise of comings and goings shall not hinder the teacher in his lecture, the steps and floors are fitted with matting, and the doors, which close themselves, are covered with cloth in the rabbets. In just the same way care is taken that the rolling of carts and coaches in the street shall not disturb the attention of the listeners, for the whole building of the auditorium is separated from the outer walls of the house by a narrow corridor, from which four entrances have been constructed. When experiments have to be made in darkness, the window above is covered by a shutter, which can be instantaneously lifted or lowered. In order to keep the room warm in winter, copper pipes are led around it, into which is forced hot steam from a boiler downstairs in the house.

In short, neither effort nor cost has been spared, to make this auditorium into one of the most magnificent, and certainly the completest, of its kind. Near to the auditorium is a room for chemical and physical instruments and apparatus; on the same floor is also the library, with the equipping of which they were busy at the time of my departure. In the top storey are the living apartments of the professors and besides these various other rooms for large models and machines.

In this institution, besides the necessary craftsmen, two professors are employed, that is, one for chemistry and one for mechanics and physics. Both have excellent salaries. Professor Davy [Sir Humphry Davy] who teaches chemistry, seems quite to have been made for the institution: his phraseology is clear and simple, and he also possesses in a high degree the art of presenting the matter pleasantly, without thereby losing in thoroughness; added to this he has a very clear enunciation, and even his youth and his modest appearance may have contributed not a little to the increase in the number of enthusiasts for his science. A talk about the uses and applications of chemistry, with which he opened his lectures last winter, surpassed, in my opinion, everything that I had previously heard of scientific eloquence, not even excepting Fourcroy's lectures. And thus the throng of listeners of both sexes and of all classes became so great that one always had to be there in good time, in order to get a seat.

Before I close this perhaps already too extended description of the Royal Institution, I must further remark that the subscribers to it are of three kinds: shareholders, each of whom pays a subscription of 70 guineas and thereby has a share in the fixed and movable assets of the Institution: after them, life subscribers, who pay 20 guineas, and have no share in the Institution, but merely receive their tickets for the lectures and the reading rooms. Finally there are annual subscribers, who upon payment of 3 guineas have the same rights as the last-named class, but for one year only. Also foreigners, who are staying for a long or short time in London, can subscribe, and travellers, who have acquaintances among the shareholders, can get tickets from them for one or several days.

Besides this, it is part of the scheme of the Institution, to serve each and every seeker after knowledge without differentiation of class or persons. Therefore workmen from the lowest classes of the populace are also admitted to the lectures; for the comfort of themselves and others, they have their special seats. The reading rooms are open daily for the subscribers and those who have received tickets from them, and are closed at the beginning of summer. The Royal Institution also has papers printed in the form of a Journal, of which several small booklets have already appeared, which contain complete information about the beginning, progress, and objects of the Institution.

The Royal Society, or the English academy of sciences, is too well known to need any description here. I therefore merely remark that the members of the society meet every Thursday evening from eight till nine, from the beginning of November until Spring. A foreigner who is acquainted with a member is easily admitted to these sessions; he has only to have himself announced before the start of the meeting by a member, who enters his own and his friend's name in a book, because a member cannot take more than one friend with him, to avoid crowding. Last winter a part of the membership, under the chairmanship of the permanent President, Joseph Banks, or in his absence, under the Vice-President, William Hamilton, foregathered for luncheon on every meeting day in a tavern near to Somerset House. Here also foreigners could be introduced by the members, and once or twice I took part with much pleasure in this learned meal, which also has a certain value for the unlearned. The Society also has a good library, and a museum of instruments and natural curiosities.

The British Museum is perhaps one of the richest collections which exists anywhere. It consists of several private collections, partly purchased by Parliament, and partly presented to the Museum. The number of rare books, manuscripts, antiquities, coins, natural history specimens, and curiosities of every kind which is preserved here, is so considerable that one can spend weeks examining them; it is only a pity that one misses in the whole thing an order and coherence which makes the Museum in the Paris Botanical Garden so instructive to the seeker after knowledge, and so comprehensible to the amateur. What most engaged my attention in this museum was the mineral collection which was bought a few years ago by Mr Hatchett.

13

c

It contains several fine specimens, and is assembled with an expenditure and a selectivity which one can expect from a capable and knowledgeable man. Mr Hatchett had originally followed the system of Werner in the display; the collection was, however, recently re-arranged by Count Bournon according to his own system, of which more is said below. Perhaps that system was not quite adequate for the arrangement of a collection made by a chemist, and which also probably contains several products which are more remarkable on account of their analysis than of their form. Among the rare specimens there is especially a little piece of the species of mineral in which Mr Hatchett discovered his new metal, columbium [niobium]. This, like a few other small pieces, which served for the discovery, he obtained in chance fashion from America, and neither for collections nor for further chemical investigation has it been possible to obtain any more of it. The mineral in which columbium is contained has much similarity to tantalite; the metal itself also has certain properties which approach those of Mr Ekeberg's tantalum, as can easily be noted in the treatises which have appeared about these two metals. This is still further corroborated by a few preliminary experiments which Mr Hatchett has made with some small pieces of tantalum which were sent to me by Mr Ekeberg.

Among the rarest minerals in the museum, which, however, do not belong in this collection, must be counted various fragments of statues, and some vessels of granite, porphyry, basalt, etc, which have recently come from Egypt, and among which a bathtub is especially remarkable. It is over 6 feet long, 3 to 4 feet deep and as wide and consists of a green and red pebble breccia or puddingstone, of which I have not yet seen specimens in any collection. Equally, Mr Hatchett, who has seen the most important collections of Europe, found no fossil which compares with this mineral.

In the fine collection of antiquities which the late Sir William Hamilton made in Naples and presented to the museum, I noticed something peculiar about the Etruscan basins of earthenware: that they were specifically lighter than any other vessels of stone or clay. Some of these basins were imitated in Staffordshire, and afterwards, by means of a coat of paint, made so similar to the genuine antiques, that they could only be distinguished from them by the weight. Does this arise from the clay which the ancients used here, or from an addition of volcanic ash of pumice, coke, or the like? When broken these vessels almost have the appearance of a strongly sun-dried blue clay.

Besides a great quantity of household articles and weapons, which belong to this collection, and which give us an idea of the progress of the ancients in the art of metalworking, there are also to be found here similar collections from all parts of the world and from more or less cultured peoples, which likewise deserved consideration. Some small iron arrows, forged by negroes in the neighbourhood of Sierra Leone, similar to those which I had earlier seen in the possession of Mr Adam Afzelius in Uppsala, bear witness to the skill of the workers and to their ingenuity in making them deadly.

The British Museum is open daily for three to four hours, except on Saturdays and Sundays, and for a few weeks in the year, when it is entirely closed. Known persons, who wish to use the library or the collections for study however, have unrestricted entry under certain conditions.

The Leverian Museum. Although this cannot actually be counted among the national institutions, since it belongs to a private citizen who keeps it open throughout the year for the moderate price of one shilling per person, it yet deserves mention next to the British Museum on account of its extent and its public interest. It contains, besides a pleasing natural history department, many collections of every kind, more, however, as curiosities than for systematic study. The mineral department, in which there are several valuable specimens, is merely arranged to please the eye. Thus one finds the finest marble and quartz crystals, garnets, pyrites, etc, placed together in groups on stands in glass cases, without any kind of mineralogical classification, while on the other hand several new and interesting minerals are entirely missing.

Among the scientific institutes of London the *Mineralogical Society* deserves a distinguished place, although it is less well known than the previously mentioned establishments. The object of this society extends not only to the scientific characteristics of minerals, but also to the application of the same in agriculture, manufacture, and handicraft. Perhaps I shall be able in the future to say something more about the organisation of this society, and I thus only remark here, that several good treatises by its members can be found in Tilloch's *Philosophical Magazine*.

Beside the mineral collections already considered, there are several other important, and from the scientific viewpoint interesting, collections which belong to individuals. The first of these is that of Mr Charles Greville, because it is not only the richest and most complete in London, but also perhaps in the world. The first foundation of this collection was purchased by the well-known Baron von Born in Vienna; it has, however, subsequently been enriched with several thousand specimens, partly by Count Bournon, who has already had it under his supervision for some years, and who, at Mr Greville's expense, buys from the mineral dealers and at auctions, everything that can serve for its completion, and partly also by the consignments which Mr Greville receives from his friends in several countries in Europe and other parts of the world.

Since the less important pieces have this year been rejected, and partly auctioned off, partly given away, the collection consists of about 11,000 specimens, which are arranged according to Count Bournon's own system, details of which will be given in the Count's rationalised catalogue, now in preparation. [J. L. de Bournon, *Catalogue de la Collection Minéralogique du Compte de Bournon* (London, 1813)] It would take up too much space to describe this collection; I will therefore only mention a few facts which can give some idea of it. All the mineral cupboards and cases are of mahogany, and the latter are fitted with glass lids, which can be easily opened and closed. Instead of the usual cardboard boxes, each particular specimen lies in a thin turned wooden box, so that the specimen can be removed from the case and observed, without touching it. These fittings alone cost Mr Greville £800 sterling. Several specimens cost 5, 10, to 15 guineas and more to buy. A piece of ruby silver ore of unusually regular crystallisation, but only weighing a few ounces, was last summer purchased at an auction for 16 guineas. Of still greater value are several specimens which Mr Greville has received as gifts, among which is a tourmaline which an English ambassador got as a present from the king of Ava. It weighs several pounds and is as large as a hat-block, and it is easy to judge its value when one knows that specimens of this mineral as large as pigeons' eggs may easily cost 10 to 15 guineas at mineral dealers. A lumachella which Mr Greville received from Prince Kaunitz in Vienna, likewise scarcely has its equal in size and beauty.

Besides such individual specimens, there are in this collection the most complete sets of precious stones, rough as well as cut. Of diamonds, for example, there are over a hundred varieties, large and small, among which a blue and a yellow, both set in one ring and weighing several carats, stand out particularly. Among the other precious stones—sapphire, ruby, etc—there are various ones of high value in sets of several hundred variations. Emerald in its matrix, several varieties of the earth in which diamonds are usually found, and similar rare things, are here in abundance. Besides that, the collection is so complete that almost no mineral is missing. If this collection were to be valued according to the scale of charges usually paid for large collections, and in accordance with which the Emperor Napoleon had one purchased in 1801 for the Museum of the Botanical Garden in Paris for 150,000 livres, then it would certainly be worth £25,000 sterling. In this connection, the collection has acquired a special value of its own through the arrangement by the Count Bournon, the progress of crystallisation, the colours, and in fact the whole chain of external characteristics, which distinguish the minerals, and give rise to their various classifications, being so clearly set out before the eyes. It seems, however, also to prove that all our systems are to be regarded as mere guides and expedients, and that a great many factors are still missing, before we get to know the great system of Nature, and the dividing lines which she has determined for each and every species.

Mr Greville is indeed himself an expert, but on account of his high position at Court and as a member of the Privy Council, he can devote himself to science only as an amateur and patron. Because of this, however, he is all the more deserving of esteem. It is a gain for science, that he has given Count Bournon the opportunity to develop his knowledge, whereby simultaneously this estimable refugee is supported in his misfortune, and through him experts and amateurs have more frequent opportunities to see the collection. It is open to everyone who comes to Mr Greville with good recommendations. I spent several days at his country house at Paddington Green, and almost every Sunday midday one could meet there a select company of mineralogists and natural historians, among which were occasionally Lord Webb Seymour, brother of the Duke of

Somerset, a Russian Prince Baretinskon, the Portuguese minister, Souza, etc. I include this merely as proof that the sciences, here as elsewhere in civilised countries, unite persons of unequal rank and fortune, of different nationality, in spite of differing political opinions.

Besides this collection, Count Bournon has two others under his supervision. One belongs to a Sir John St. Aubin; it is not so complete as that of Mr Greville, but yet contains a quantity of fine specimens, particularly from Cornwall and several districts of England. Sir Abraham Hume owns the other collection and it is situated farther out on his estate some miles from London. I have not seen it, but I was told that it contains several interesting specimens from both Indies.

Among the smaller, but rather good mineral collections are: (1) that of Mr Richard Phillips, Georges Church Yard, which deserves to be seen especially on account of its fine copper specimens, rich tin ores, etc, from Cornwall. Mr Phillips is himself a mineralogist and chemist, and one is received by him with the simple and unassuming courtesy which distinguishes an enlightened Quaker.

(2) Mr Sowerby's collection, Mead Place, Lambeth, contains a great many crystals, and is daily enriched with new kinds. Mr Sowerby is an engraver, and has actually founded this collection for the purpose of a work on the minerals of England which he wants to publish, and thereby apparently intends to refute the assertion of many, that one cannot give a complete conception of the outer appearance of minerals through engravings and colouring. At least, I recognised at first glance various kinds whose differentiation on paper I had formerly held to be impossible. This, like Mr Phillips' collection, is arranged on Haun's system.

(3) the collection of Doctor Crichton, and (4) that of Doctor Babington. The former is particularly rich in Scottish minerals, and the latter, which however, I had not the

opportunity of seeing, is said to contain various Irish objects, which are otherwise not frequently met with.

Besides this, there are several mineral dealers in London, who must be visited by a travelling miner. One often finds in their shops specimens of high value on account of their beautiful appearance or their rarity and novelty. One goes in, as in every other shop, and even if one buys nothing, but is only known as an honest man, and does not betray too great an ignorance, one can spend several hours there, observe every specimen at pleasure, and ask all manner of questions, without having anything to fear. Here, as with every other business in England, with the exception of Jews and receivers of stolen goods, it is also the rule not to bargain. The honesty of the seller and the buyer's knowledge of the value of the goods is assumed. In the honesty of the former one is seldom deceived, for he is just as much concerned about his credit as the customer is unwilling to betray his ignorance. Thereby one avoids on both sides the disgraceful practice of deceit which is so general here and in France, especially among the more cultured parts of the nation. The best mineral dealers in London at present are: Mr Forster, Gerard Street, Soho; Mr Man, Tavistock Street, Covent Garden; Mr Latham, Long Acre; Mr Heslop, Chiswell Street, Finsbury Square; and Mr Moore, Great Turnstile, Holborn. These also deal in birds, snails, cut stones—in short, with all kinds of natural curiosities and oddities. With the Jews and in so-called second-hand shops one also meets with good objects by chance, but one must examine the goods closely, and bargain well.

In recalling the mineral collections and their proprietors with whom I have experienced so many pleasant hours in London, I had almost forgotten to say wherein one of the foremost experts and patrons of the sciences, Sir Joseph Banks, earns the greatest respect and honour, that is to say, through the generosity with which he permits everyone to use his library of natural history and his collections. The former is open daily from 10 in the morning until 3 in the afternoon, and one of the librarians is always present, to give any information which may be required. Known persons can without difficulty borrow books for a longer or shorter period, and they are so accustomed to law and order here, that they never even ask for a receipt or a slip for the return of the book. A Swede, who may not perhaps want to take advantage of this opportunity, will do well occasionally to visit Sir Joseph's library, because he will have the opportunity of meeting here our worthy and learned countryman Dryander, who is now the first librarian.[2] The latter not only knows London well, but takes pleasure in serving his countrymen with such information as is useful and necessary to a traveller. Besides this, at certain times of the year, Sir Joseph holds so-called Tea Assemblies every Sunday, where, so soon as one has been introduced, one has free entry, and meets here from 6 to 10 o'clock in the evening a learned company of all classes and nations.

Chapter 2

The South-West

AFTER I HAD SPENT THE WINTER MONTHS IN PART IN THE examination of the above-mentioned institutions, and had not only made a good circle of acquaintances, but also obtained some practice in the language of the country, I decided in February to undertake a journey to the ironworks. However, I soon found that it was extremely difficult to obtain the information necessary for this purpose. Neither natives, who dealt in iron, nor proprietors of ironworks, of whom I had already got to know several, could indicate to me exactly which route I would have to take in order to see the most and the largest ironworks, what difficulties a foreigner would encounter in his inquiries, etc. It is true that General Consul Grill, who is always very ready to serve his travelling fellow-countrymen, had promised me his recommendation to the famous foundry owner, Mr Crawshay in Wales, but since I subsequently heard that the latter had the previous year refused a Swedish tourist entry to his works, I could not hope for anything better for myself. Despairingly I sought information about ironworks in the guides and travel-books, of which a great number are available, and more of which are published daily about certain districts of England. These contain more or less wearisome descriptions of churches, castles, antiquities, views, etc, which indeed could be edifying for other tourists, but were of no use at all to me. I had therefore almost decided to go straight to Scotland, where I was provided by a friend with introductions to some ironworks, among them one of the largest, belonging to John Wilson & Son of London. Meantime I came to speak to Mr Greville of the object of my tour, and of the difficulty, that I could not usefully undertake it owing to the lack of adequate information. He soon helped me out of my difficulty, and not only offered me introductions to the largest ironworks of the kingdom, but also gave me an extract from his mineralogical notes which he had collected on a tour in south Wales and a part of Cornwall.

It is true that my actual destination was not Cornwall, where there are no ironworks, but because Mr Greville represented to me that a journey there would be interesting in several respects, and at the same time suggested as a travelling companion a French Ingénieur des Mines, M. Bonnard, whose acquaintance I had already made through General Andreoffy, I thought that this detour was acceptable in order afterwards to be able to see the things which were the principal object of my tour, in good company and under such good patronage. I therefore postponed my journey for a few days, and meantime collected serviceable information from all sides. Among the books which can serve the tourist as a guide, I found only in Aikin's *Letters* some information about the places where there are mines and certain factories. After that I provided myself with a guidebook which contained the distances between all places and towns, the advertisements of the best inns, and some incomplete information about the noteworthy places to be found on the way. One must of necessity be provided with these two books as well as a good map of England, for at a distance of a few miles from the most noteworthy place, one can probably ask a hundred persons the way to it, without finding anyone who knows anything about it. Besides that it is necessary to be able to show the names, after which one is inquiring, in printed or written form, for the English themselves often do not know how a name is pronounced in different places.

After we had been provided with the necessary letters of introduction, partly by Mr Greville himself, partly by his friends, among others by the Duke of Devonshire, we left London on 1 March 1803. In order to gain time, especially since there is little of interest for a miner on the way to Cornwall, until he comes into Devonshire, we decided to go direct to Exeter, about 27 Swedish miles [1 Swedish mile = 6·644 statute miles] from the capital. In this connection, I must remark, for the information of other tourists, that when one books a seat in a coach from London to a distant place, it is necessary to inquire minutely at the coach-office, where one is registered and makes the payment, about the quality of the coach and by which route it goes. If one travels with the Royal Mail, which belongs to the Post Office and is subject to certain regulations, this is not necessary; we, however, for the sake of economy, booked places on another coach, which was said to be equipped just like the Royal Mail coaches, and to be able to take just as many passengers, although it would arrive in Exeter a few hours later.

When we arrived in Picadilly, where we were supposed to board, we found that the coach had turned into a 'long coach' for twelve persons, and which was packed so full of passengers that I was obliged to speak to the coachman in a serious tone before two gentlemen, who actually had to sit up above on the roof, made place for us. Either this was an error in the coach office, or it had been done on purpose; however, the consequence was that my travelling companion and I had to make a detour of more than three Swedish miles via Bath, where we did not want to go at all. One travels, however, better in these country coaches than in any kind of Swedish hired vehicle, and the only problem is the necessity to take good care of one's luggage. For these coaches make exchanges, and because they convey a great number of packages and suitcases, which are to be quickly unloaded at certain stops, there is a real danger of losing one or the other piece in the hurry. If, however, one affixes one's name and address to each article, one is certain to get goods lost in this way back sooner or later. Although we did not here travel in such good company as on the better post coaches, we had in the main lost nothing, because we came in good time to Bath, where we caught a Flying Coach (light vehicle) which brought us punctually to Exeter.

We found on the way nothing more remarkable (from our point of view) than a few small canals in the neighbourhood of Bath, which flow into the Kennet and Avon canal connecting the two rivers of the same names, and opening up communication between the Severn and Thames estuaries. It is said that on one of these canals Mr Weldon's invention, of bringing the boats into watertight cases instead of the usual locks, and letting them down to the lower stream, is to be introduced. A great quantity of coals were transported and unloaded on these canals, but I do not know for certain whether there are coalmines nearby, or whether the coal has been brought here from a distance.

Between Bath and Exeter the country is very hilly, and in the highlands, which are throughout of the second order, several kinds of stone outcrop, which are cut and used for building. Near the town of Wells in Somersetshire large slabs of a black limestone were cut and polished by hand into gravestones and the like.

Half a Swedish mile from Exeter, near the village of Pine [Pinhoe] are some pyrolusite mines. The deepest which I saw was merely some 8 fathoms, and worked out; the manganese ore occurs in nests in a red, greasy, half-hard, and foliated clay. The work is done here with large pickaxes, such as are used in repairing the streets in London, and the ore is brought to the surface without any special skill in large lumps, which are then broken up, sorted, and washed in waterbutts installed for the purpose. In the washing, which is done by women and children, and by means of which the red clay, which is often sintered together with the ore, is supposed to be separated, much of the ore is lost. However, the manganese ore is found in some nodules so pure that it does not need to be washed, and this kind, wherein there are often fine needle-shaped crystals, is sold specially and at a high price. Near these mines and everywhere around here there are large mounds which consist partly of argillite, partly of a reddish so-called gravel, or chalk grains with rounded corners enclosed in a reddish clay, which seems merely to be a variation of that in which the manganese ore occurs. This kind of gravel also comes to light at greater or lesser depths in the mines.

A few miles from Exeter, towards the sea, around the little town of Neuton Bushel [Newton Bushel is the former name of Newton Abbot] the district is low and enclosed by hills, which consist partly of a light grey, coarse-grained and not very hard granite, partly of a dense, grey-black or quite black limestone, with interspersed veins and nodules of a white spathic chalk. The granite, which likewise occurs in several variations of colour and texture on Dartmoor and in several places in Devonshire and Cornwall, seems here, as everywhere, to form the basis of the later chalk and slate hills. At one of these hills, near to Neuton Bushel, lime is burnt in specially erected furnaces of two types of construction. The one kind was similar to our blast-furnace shafts, was 18 feet deep and rather wider in proportion. The other kind of limekiln, which is more frequently met with in England, was only 14 to 15 feet deep, and had the form of an inverted cone. How the burning is accomplished in these furnaces, will be discussed below.

Near to the road, before one comes to Neuton, and indeed in the above-mentioned small plain, there are some

clay-pits, partly for an earthenware factory nearby at Bovey
Tracey, partly for factories of the same kind in Stafford,
Worcestershire, and at several places in England. This
clay is of two kinds, either black or grey-brown, but both
become white, or more accurately, yellowish-white, on
firing. Above the best clay lies another mixed with sand,
which is used for bricks, and between which small, almost
horizontal, one- to two-inch thick coal seams occur. In one
such claypit of eight to ten feet depth, which, however,
consisted mainly of good clay, several layers of the inferior
kind were visible, the thickness of which varied with the
rise or fall of the earth's surface.

Nearer to Bovey Tracey the plain changes into a peat-
bog, which, just at the point to the north where it lies
against the heights, contains a great deal of fossilised wood,
the trunks and roots of which are found at a little depth
below the surface. A few stone's throws higher up runs a
deposit of a sort of half-carbonised coal, which carried
clear indications of an overturned and destroyed forest.
The fresh timber, which is dug up by the country people
around Bovey, is partially used as firewood, and partly for
various rough works of joinery, such as tables, chairs, and
the like. Most of it is oak, black, very dense, and quite like
that which is dug up below Akersjd near the Trollhatta in
Sweden. The thickness of the coal seam, which falls at a
few degrees towards the plain, increases with depth. It is
said that it is about 60 feet thick at its greatest depth,
counting in several layers of clay and thin deposits of true
coal, which occur within it, the former some feet and the
latter a few inches thick. The mine was driven entirely
underground, and was greatly inconvenienced by water,
which could only at certain times be kept down to the
sump by a steam engine with a fourteen-inch cylinder and
two pumps of 8 and $5\frac{1}{2}$ inches diameter. The coal is used
as fuel in households, for lime-burning, and for certain

operations in the pottery nearby. For other work in this factory, hard coal must be used, which is brought up from the sea by means of a small canal. A mill was also connected to the steam engine, in order to grind burnt flint, which is used here as a glaze. This mill consisted of a cylindrical basin of granite, 12 inches deep and 6 or 7 feet in diameter, in which two stones on edge were driven round in a circle; they moved on an axle, which was placed at right angles to the main pillar, and the latter received a circular movement by means of a connecting rod from the steam engine. Near the mines and at the factory a few houses were built of peat; this was well dried and cut in longish rectangles, like our largest building bricks. Some of these houses had a lower storey of quarried stone, upon which was laid a two-feet thick peat wall between light timber frameworks. My guidebook said that if peat houses were built with three-feet thick walls, a permanent roof could be placed thereon without timbering. I afterwards saw such houses in other places, which, however, were seldom inhabited, but merely used as stables, etc. They are very warm and last several years. The peat moor is said now to lie nearly six feet above the highest water level. No one knows when it was under water, but old people in the place say that it is now more dried out than in their youth.

In order to get to Dartmoor, which is considered to be one of the highest ridges of hills in this part of England, we took our way to Moreton Hampstead, a small town between Exeter and Plymouth. The way there goes from Bovey uphill for a couple of Swedish miles, albeit this climb varies with steep and long slopes. The mountains consist here partly of the above-mentioned grey granite, partly of a coarser kind, like the Swedish, in which the feldspar is predominant, only with the difference that the Swedish is usually denser and more red, but this is lighter and greyish. On the side of a hill, not far from Moreton

Hampstead, a substance is dug out which in appearance is exactly the same as a pulverised plumbago or graphite, but which was found on accurate chemical analysis to be a kind of iron ore, like the *Eisenmann* of the Germans. This mineral, which is here called 'Shining ore', is sold at six guineas a ton, and a great deal of it is sent to London and other places in England, where it is used for various purposes instead of plumbago or graphite. It is especially used for the cleaning and polishing of certain parts of cast iron, such as steam cylinders, hotplates, etc, which not only thereby receive a fine appearance, but are also protected from rust.

From Moreton Hampstead to Plymouth one passes over the highest part of Dartmoor. Over a stretch of more than four miles, where the slope begins to go down to the sea, the land is little inhabited, without woods or cultivation, and in several places has the awful appearance of a wilderness. Over a Swedish mile one encounters scarcely one or two miserable huts, which presumably serve the herdsmen as shelters at certain seasons; however, when I travelled through here no sign of a living being was to be seen, apart from rabbits, which grub up and undermine the soil everywhere. In this district tin mines lie near the road, which are now very little worked, but bear witness to an earlier more intensive operation. Near to Plymouth, at a place named Two Bridges, there are likewise some unimportant tin mines and a small smelting works; however, the company had begun to open a gallery, whereby they hope to extend the working here considerably. The usual type of rock in these mines is the above-mentioned grey granite, but close to the ore other sorts break through, among which a reddish one, whose appearance falls between zeolite and feldspar, and another, yellow-green, like serpentine, but much harder, deserve to be more closely investigated.

The greater part of this ridge of hills belongs to the

Prince of Wales, who is now beginning to sell or to lease out small parcels of it. In one place a few hundred acres were enclosed for timber plantations; but even if this undertaking should be successful, it is not very dangerous for our iron manufacture, so long as the need for timber in England must increase rather than decrease. Anyway, the planting of timber is the only way of aiding this district, where the costs of transporting coal and building material up from the sea are too heavy. The height of Dartmoor above the sea must be considerable, for the ground there was everywhere covered with snow, and the ice on the puddles was so strong that one could walk over it, whereas at Plymouth, where we arrived on the same day, little snow and ice was to be seen. From these heights the harbour town of Plymouth is supplied with fresh water, which is conducted for several English miles, either in open ditches or through iron pipes.

We took up our night quarters near the docks at Plymouth, from where we wanted to go the next morning by water to Torpoint, and from there direct to St Austell in Cornwall. We should both very much have liked to see over the shipyards and some of the buildings attached thereto, but this is permitted to a foreigner only with great difficulty, and a mere attempt to do it would, in the present-day state of affairs, have been imprudent. However, the next morning we passed between the warships lying in the harbour, and somewhat higher up, from the landing place, we had the most beautiful view of Plymouth Sound, the town, the harbour, the fortifications, and the neighbouring district, over which Dartmoor with its white mantle of snow seemed to rise up into the clouds.

Between Torpoint and St Austell, which is a good day's journey, one passes through a district which is fairly cultivated and stocked with deciduous timber. The mountains and uplands are, however, more interesting to the landscape painter than to the miner, for before one approaches St Austell, they consist merely of a shale with a greater or less admixture of pebbles, which occasionally passes from pure argillite into the so-called killas, or Cornwall gneiss, in innumerable variations of colour and grain. In various places where the road had been cut some fathoms deep through the shale rocks, one could observe these variations very well. In the towns and villages no trace of important manufactures could be seen. The towns are small and compared with other towns of England narrow and badly built, and perhaps only remarkable on account of their commerce in the parliamentary elections.

St Austell is a small town, with narrow and winding streets, but very lively on account of the nearby tin mines and smelting works. We were here recommended to Mr Charles Rashleigh, who not only possesses important mines, but is also generally known here on account of his great patriotic undertakings. Thus, for example, Mr Rashleigh thought that a better harbour was necessary in the neighbourhood of St Austell; to this end he had already ten years ago selected a suitable place for it, of which the Prince of Wales, as Duke of Cornwall, was landlord. By an agreement concluded with the Prince, which was afterwards confirmed by Act of Parliament, Mr Rashleigh acquired for a certain sum of money the complete right of ownership in this place and in a stretch of land round about it. Eight years ago the cultivation of this area, which at that time was an unfruitful wilderness, was begun, and now some hundreds of acres of land are enclosed by stone walls and divided into farms, which last year (1801) brought in between £1 and £3 sterling per acre, and some of which are leased out at £7 and more. Besides that the owner has here founded a pleasing estate, with a fine house, lawns, and plantations, which were already completely in order. For the security of the harbour, which is named Charlestown after the builder, a high wall against the sea was put in, and several docks were founded for loading and unloading vessels and for the repair of the same. Several small ships and boats were being built here, and others were being overhauled. For the benefit of seafarers a large inn was furnished, and a long alley with little houses for the workpeople was laid out, to say nothing of the warehouse, brickworks, and limekilns.

Mr Rashleigh, who was unable to accompany us on our excursion to the mines and smelting works, had already before our arrival spoken to a manager (or, as they are called here, a Captain of Mines) Phillips, and asked him to go with us. This Mr Phillips is very skilled in his business; besides that he knows the district, and takes pleasure in giving tourists any kind of information for which they ask. I shall have an opportunity in the future particularly to describe the tin-stone mines and the smelting process used there, so I shall here only remark that in this district the three principal variations of the tin-stone, and the accordingly modified working methods, which occur in the whole country, are encountered. He who undertakes a journey to Cornwall only as a mineralogist or miner will likewise lose nothing if he makes a tour of Truro, Penryn, Marazion, Penzance, St Ives, and St Columb, near which towns there are many copper and tin mines. One must then have introductions to Mr Rashleigh of Monabilly, brother of the above-mentioned gentleman of the same name, who possesses one of the richest collections of minerals in England, particularly of Cornwall. Two Quakers, William Jenkin and Silvanus James in Redruth, likewise deserve to be visited, because they know the country very well, and also own collections, and will either themselves do business or give advice about mineral dealers.

A few English miles from St Austell, near a St Stephens church, the white fireproof clay, which is not only used in several districts of England and Scotland for the genuine porcelain wares which were recently introduced and which have come rapidly into fashion, but also in the great Wedgwood Etruria factory in Staffordshire, etc, is dug out and levigated. Near the clay pit, only somewhat higher up, the white, translucent, and grainy feldspar is quarried, which is mixed with the porcelain mass in order to bring about an incomplete fusion during the firing, whereby, without further additions, it receives a glazed surface, and becomes translucent at the edges. These two substances seem to me to be very similar to those which I had formerly seen in the manufactories of Sèvres and Paris; the latter get their materials from Limoges under the names of kaolin and petuntse. Because the discovery of the clay near St Stephens actually led to the first foundation of the famous Etruria and the invention of the factory-made articles, which still daily bring such enormous sums into England, an extended description of this in many respects remarkable product may not be out of place.

The clay itself, which occurs in a low-lying area or in a small valley enclosed by fairly high mountains, and which consists mostly of killas, partly of a decomposed granite, is found just below the surface soil, where it is dug out with spades, eight to nine feet deep (at least, they have not needed up till now to go any deeper). If a lump of it is laid on a spade to dry for an hour, it takes on completely the appearance of a light grey granite, which is more or less sprinkled with chalky water, and the vertical cuttings of the clay pits look more like a hewn granite wall than a clay mass. Also the clay here constitutes only a part of the whole mass, and can be regarded merely as a medium wherein the three constituents of granite, quartz, feldspar, and mica are enveloped in such proportions that the substance upon drying takes on the appearance of real granite. Now this substance is either, according to the opinion of some mineralogists, to be regarded as decomposed granite, and the pure clay as decomposed feldspar, or (which according to my ideas and those of several Englishmen is equally possible), it has never been compounded, but has merely contained the foundation material (prevailing constituents) of a granite, whose combination Nature could not complete on account of hindrances: this can in itself be immaterial. The main thing is, to know how this product is used, and this comes about in the following way: After the substance has been brought out in lumps as large as the spade can carry, it is taken to washing troughs and drying houses some distance off. Here one or more lumps are thrown simultaneously into a trench or wash-basin in the ground, with running water, and there crushed with the spade, whereupon, during the continuous stirring the pure clay is separated and washed away with the water to the settling house. When the trench in which this operation is carried out is filled with granite sand, it is cleared out with the spade, and in the same simple fashion, the water is directed to and fro, as necessary.

The clay which has been washed in this way then goes through several settling ponds, set one above the other, until it finally comes into the lower pit of the drying house. The latter is built up of granite by one of the claypits itself, and is provided at the gable end with small holes one above the other, through which the clear water is allowed to run off as the clay sinks. When all the water has run away, the clay is allowed to lie for a few more days, so that it sinks still further, and gains consistency, after which it is lifted out in large cubic pieces, set out in the drying house, and, when it is thoroughly dried, packed in casks. It is now in the highest degree fine and pure, and can be used for porcelain mixes without further treatment.

The feldspar or petuntse, which is used in porcelain manufacture, is no less remarkable. It occurs in the same valley, but higher up and in solid rock. It is found, so far as can be perceived by eye, in a grey, half-hard granite mass, in which quartz and mica are noticeably poor, and in which the feldspar seems to displace one or both. I could not find out exactly how this substance is prepared before it is added to the porcelain mix, although I do not believe that there is anything secret about it, but as an article of commerce it occurs in larger and smaller lumps, whose sorting, on account of a granitic material which occurs in the same quarry, demands much practice. The only difference which I could detect between that which was kept and that which was rejected, was in the colour and in a tiny admixture of mica and quartz. The above-mentioned lumps of feldspar are packed in casks, just like the clay, and then taken overland to Charlestown, from there shipped to Liverpool, and finally dispatched over the inland canals to several factories in Staffordshire, Worcester, Shropshire, etc.

In order to avoid a detour of rather more than twenty Swedish miles from St Austell to the ironworks in South Wales, and at the same time to see a part of England which is otherwise seldom visited by tourists, Mr Greville had advised M. Bonnard and myself to make our way through Bodmin and Launceston in Cornwall, from there through Okehampton, Hatherleigh, Torrington, and Barnstaple in Devonshire, to a little harbour on the Bristol Channel, named Ilfracombe, from which latter place a packet boat departs twice or three times a week for Swansea. The towns named, except Barnstaple, which has tanneries and some large weaving mills, are small and have a mean appearance, with few or no manufactures. Also the land over this whole stretch is not much cultivated, and even though one here and there encounters places of unusual cultivation, the other districts are more unfruitful by comparison. It is certainly very hilly, and the rock-types consist partly of several kinds of shale, or so-called slate, partly of rocks of chalky or granitic nature, which latter rise perceptibly above the others.

The hills here, with the exception of Dartmoor, which appears on the right between Launceston and Okehampton as a high, flat ridge of hills, rise up in more or less pointed peaks, whose summits are fairly similar to the Swedish high Fjällen. The valleys formed by these hills are also more cup-shaped than in most of the mountain regions of Sweden, and almost have the appearance of dried-up basins. I mention this observation now, because I first made it here, but I believe that I afterwards remarked that this situation is general in the English mountains, with the exception of those of granite, which I met with nowhere else but in the neighbourhood of Dartmoor and Exmoor.

In the whole region from Exeter through Cornwall and Devonshire, few houses were roofed with tiles, except in the seaports; they were in general built of a hard slate, of limestone, or of both kinds of stone set in clay. These houses, which are inhabited by the poorer classes of people on the land, and are called cobhouses, belong among the most miserable dwellings which one can see, but the walls are usually planted around with a kind of tree (ivy), whose branches and foliage cover a great part of the house and give it almost the appearance of a bower. On the way between Bodmin and Launceston we saw some limekilns of the form already described.

In case our unusual route should excite mistrust, or our voyage to Swansea run into difficulties, we were provided with letters of introduction from a member of parliament for Barnstaple to Mr Gribble and Son of that place. These were delivered immediately after our arrival, and we were given another letter from Mr Gribble to one of his friends in Ilfracombe.

Ilfracombe is a little place, but has a good harbour which is often visited by ships, some of which want to go up to Bristol, but which arrive in the roadsteads through error or currents. A few English miles away lies Combe Martin where ironstone is supposed to be found, which is now and then mined and shipped to South Wales.

The packet boat mentioned, with which we wanted to cross over to Swansea, was now over there, and had not been able to return for several days on account of storms. After we had vainly awaited it for a couple of days, we hired for five guineas a little vessel of the kind generally used for smuggling, and here called skiffs, in which we made the crossing in barely three hours. When one agrees upon such a sea voyage, one must lay down the express condition in advance, that several passengers shall not be allowed without special permission. Because we had omitted to come to an agreement with the skipper about this, we got an Irish officer for company, who legally would have had to contribute to our charter fee.

On our arrival at Swansea the tide had already gone out so far that we could only approach within a Swedish quarter-mile of the harbour. We were therefore landed at a place called Oystermouth, from whence we had our goods transported half a Swedish mile to the town on a cart hauled by four oxen, for seven English shillings.

Chapter 3

South Wales

MR GREVILLE HAD GIVEN US SEVERAL LETTERS OF INTRODUC-
tion to Swansea, some to proprietors of the copperworks
and coalmines here, some to persons who had time to be
of service to us as guides, also one to one of the leading
businessmen of the town, Dr Collins, who is here Port-
reeve, or senior harbourmaster. In England one cannot,
without having business of the highest importance, visit
anyone in the afternoon. If, however, one arrives at a place
to which one is addressed, towards evening, it is necessary,
to gain time, to send off one's letters of introduction with
a note asking when one can call. Usually one is then in-
vited to breakfast on the following day, or to call at a
certain hour. If one has several letters, it is necessary, to
avoid confusion and difficulties, to send off only one at a
time and wait for an answer, unless one can dispose of the
recipient's time at pleasure.

Dr Collins, who had received our letter on the previous
evening, honoured us with a visit on the next morning,
and offered himself to accompany us to the harbour, which
is noteworthy on account of its spaciousness and the works
which have been built and which are still in hand, for the
protection of the ships. A thick wall (pier) some fathoms
high and several hundred yards long, had already been
built out into the sea in the form of a half-circle, and provided at the outer end with a lighthouse, by means of
which the seafarers who must seek out the inner harbour

at night, can orient themselves. An equal if not greater wall is to be laid out from an opposite point of land, and thus within these walls will be formed a harbour for several hundred ships, which will lie here secure from all possible winds. All this is being done at the expense of the town, which a few decades ago was of little importance, but in recent years, through the rich coalmines, mines and factories in the neighbourhood, has risen to an almost unbelievable degree of prosperity. The above-mentioned harbour walls were built of a greyish-black, squared, and easily worked sandstone, which is also much used for house-building in the town and the neighbourhood. As mortar a kind of natural cement has been employed, which occurs on the opposite coast, south of Neath at a place named Aberavon. This cement is in its raw condition nothing other than a variety of limestone, which before burning is greyish-white, of a dense, brittle texture; after burning it takes on a coarse appearance, and is unsuitable for fine work or for agriculture. On the other hand it is advantageous for such buildings as are exposed to water or dampness, without needing to be mixed with anything other than sand. I have neither in Holland nor in France, where the same kind of mortar is made with an addition of trass or pozzolana, seen a more solid and faultless wall, notwithstanding that the waves of the sea beat unceasingly upon the outer side, and in storms the whole thing is soaked with a rain of salt water.

Another kind of limestone, black, fine-grained, and sometimes interspersed with white veins, which frequently occurs in the neighbourhood around Swansea, gave after burning a fine, white lime, which was not suitable for this work, but was used for whitewash and on the fields. This reminds me of various things about chalk and other mortars, which I have partly observed myself and partly heard about from others, and which may here warrant mention.

First of all, it is known in Sweden that the grey lime of Götlands and grey lime in general, is stronger (more binding) than the fine white Weissbinder lime. We further know that some of the lime of Dannemora, but especially that from Wattholma, has an unusual binding strength, which is best shown in the ponds and dykes of the mines at Dannemora; however, this stone becomes less serviceable in the mass for addition to the blast furnace as this peculiarity increases. The lime which is burnt near Hunneberg, and has been used in building the locks at Trollhätta, was very white upon complete slaking, but on the other hand not very binding, and the mortar made from this lime was, if it were not mixed with cement, fairly easily dissolved by water.

In the hills around Paris, and especially near Montmartre, a yellowish-white, gypsum-containing limestone is quarried, which becomes very white upon burning, and gives an excellent lime for house-building and for plastering walls, but it cannot be used for wet walls without an admixture of pozzolana. Thus the discovery of a limestone in the neighbourhood of Boulogne, which was made just before my departure from Paris, is considered to be very important; in appearance it is rather like that of Aberavon and according to information received, it should have the same property in mortar of withstanding water and dampness. Also in London I was told of a case which, like the foregoing, bears witness to the variable nature and properties of limestone. A farmer had used lime as a fertiliser on two of his estates. On one of them the lime had the desired effect, which in England is so generally known, of promoting the vegetation; on the other property the meadows were completely spoiled, and eventually there was a total failure of the harvest. This was all the less comprehensible, since the fields as well as the lime seemed to have the same characteristics on both farms, until a skilled chemist, Dr

Tennant, from whom I had the information, found by a proper analysis that the last-mentioned sort contained a substantial proportion of foreign matter.

All this seems sufficiently to prove, how little attention has up till now been paid to the variable nature of lime, and how unsafe are the rules for the preparation of mortar which are found in books, if one cannot obtain the same kind of lime that the author had, or does not possess enough mineralogical knowledge to draw conclusions about its properties from its outward appearance. Perhaps it would be safest if, for every purpose where ordinary lime is used, one were to assure oneself of its nature and properties by a small-scale experiment, at least until mineralogists and chemists can shed more light upon this important subject.

At the above-described harbour wall a part of the pavement was laid with slag bricks from the nearby copper works, but this is seldom done, because they can get enough stone, which is more durable.

Since I shall have the opportunity on a future occasion to describe in greater detail the coalmines and copper works, as well as the operations practised therein, I shall here merely mention a few matters which can give a general idea of the great liveliness and the principal manufactures of Swansea. I have mentioned the harbour above, which partly by Nature, partly by Art, is already in such a condition that the extensive shipping traffic no longer meets with any obstruction. In the same way I have described the building materials which, next to the rich coal seams which begin on the border of Carmarthenshire and extend through the whole of Glamorganshire and a part of Brecknock into Monmouthshire, have presumably given rise to the great industrial undertakings to be seen here. These coal seams, concerning whose situation and depth not everyone seems yet to be agreed, are nevertheless encountered in an almost unbroken chain, over a stretch of more than fifteen Swedish miles in length and three to four miles in breadth, surrounded on all sides by chalk and slate mountains. Besides sufficient coal, ironstone, sandstone, clay, and limestone for forty-two blast furnaces, of which each produces about 2,000 tons of pig-iron annually, or all together nearly 700,000 pounds, Swedish shipping weight [shippounds: 7½ shippounds = 1 ton], these seams likewise provide coal for the production of 6,000 to 7,000 tons, or nearly 50,000 shippounds of copper, which is produced at fourteen copper works around Swansea and the Neath canal, within a small district of a few Swedish square miles.

The same seams supply several alum works, porcelain factories, and a host of other coal-using establishments with coal, besides what goes to limekilns and the household requirements of the continually growing population in the towns and in the country round about, as well as several hundred thousand tons which are shipped over the River Tavey [Tawe] and the Neath Canal to Cornwall and abroad. It is remarkable that these coal deposits were little worked up till thirty to forty years ago, and that on the unfruitful and bare heathland, which still twenty years ago was merely grazed by goats, there now live thousands of people, whose work brings millions into the country, and contributes to an extraordinarily high degree to its culture and growth.

To return to Swansea, one finds near by the town on the River Tavey [Tawe] and up the Swansea Canal, as well as on the road to Neath, such a profusion of copper works, coalmines, steam engines, ponds, canals, aqueducts, and railways, that the traveller, on arrival, becomes quite undecided as to where he should first direct his attention. Also a stranger would be able to go around here for several days without being able to make order out of this chaos, if he had no one with him who knew the works, for here, just as in large towns, one seeks in vain for information from passers-by, any of whom seldom knows his nearest neighbours by name. We had therefore been recommended by Mr Greville, who knew all this and had foreseen it, to a Mr Morris, who had formerly been an important copper refiner, but who had now retired from this, and lived on his estate near a town which he had founded, named Morristown. Mr Morris, who is also Sheriff of the County, was just away on his business trips; however, we not only received all necessary information from his son and a Mr Lockwood, who owned coalmines and copper works, but we also had unrestricted admission to the latter's works, and permission to inquire about the methods of working.

On these excursions, which we made partly in the company of Mr Morris, partly with other expert companions, during our stay in Swansea, the following objects may deserve the attention of a tourist.

The shipping on the River Tavey [Tawe]. This river, which rises in Brecknockshire and flows into the Bay of Swansea, is, considered as a river, very unimportant, but is noteworthy in that first of all it partially provides the copper works, and in particular the steam engines, with the necessary water, and secondly, it is navigable for fairly large ships for some distance up from the estuary. These go up and down with the tide, and, at several landing places built along the river, take on coal or unload copper ore and other goods, which are afterwards transported farther inland over the canals or railways. The transport of coal from the nearest mines down to the ships is done over a railway specially laid for the purpose, which is laid at such a gradient that two waggons, coupled together and each loaded with a chaldron (about 13 hundredweights or 3,500 Swedish pounds) of coal, run forwards by their own weight, being restrained in their journey by a brake fitted to the rear waggon, applied by a man who travels with it to deal with the unloading. When the waggon comes down to the landing place in this way, it is run forward on to a bridge built out into the river; this has a large opening which is so made that the part of the ship to be loaded can comfortably lie centrally beneath it. The laden waggon is placed over this opening, and its bottom is opened by pulling out a pin, whereupon the coal immediately falls down into the ship. The empty waggons are afterwards coupled together in a train, and hauled up over the same way by a horse. In this manner coal is brought down from a shaft at Pentre Coalmine almost $1\frac{1}{2}$ English miles to the river. From the more distant mines the coal is first taken over such inclined railways down to the Swansea canal, where it is loaded into boats, one of which often only carries 2 to 3 tons; these boats either go over branch canals constructed for the purpose, directly to some landing place, or the coal is again transferred into the above-described waggons. Occasionally also these little boats go a whole English mile or more underground, and take on their loads in the mine itself.

The canals and aqueducts. Beside the often-mentioned, five-feet deep and ten-feet-wide Swansea canal, which stretches a few English miles up into the country beside the River Tavey [Tawe], there are several small canals and aqueducts, which partly carry the water to the surrounding works, and partly are laid out for smaller boats. Among the latter some come out of the mines, and either cross the large canals on aqueducts, or fall into them. Others are conducted to some copper works or to the places on the River Tavey [Tawe] where there are larger or smaller collecting places, where several boats at once can be unloaded comfortably. At one of the copper works such a collecting place or basin was laid out at the same level as the eaves of the roof of the building, so that the boats, which went to the coalmine a Swedish mile underground

44

on one of the small canals, could on their return empty
their loads directly into the smelting house. In other places
were aqueducts, which pass under the large canals by stone-
built culverts, either to carry the water away from the
mines, or to provide the engines and copper works with it.

The railways or roads of iron. These, which one now
encounters in the whole of England, often some Swedish
miles long, and of all dimensions, here run all over the
place between the canals and works. Most of them were
built for waggons of 1 chaldron lading, which either run
by their own weight in the manner previously described,
or several, coupled together are drawn by a horse. Although
these ways are all alike at a first glance, they are actually of
two kinds. The one kind are called railroads or railways
and consist of iron bars 2 to 3 inches wide, which are completely smooth on the inner and upper edges, but which
can have any desired form on the under edge and the outer
side. The waggons which run on them have flanges on the
inside edges of the wheels, so that the waggon, while the
wheel rolls unobstructed on the bars, is held on the road
by means of these flanges. The other kind are called tramroads or tramways. The track, in which the wheel here
runs, has a turned-up flange on the outer side, and the
wheel is like that of an ordinary wheelbarrow.[3]

The steam engines. It is not too much to say that these
engines are as common in England, and are found in far
greater numbers, as are water- and windmills with us; also
they are encountered, just like the latter, in all possible
sizes, of better or worse construction. Those around Swansea, in comparison to those which I afterwards saw in
Wales and Shropshire, at Newcastle and in Manchester,
have no distinction other than the novelty that so many of
them are used in one place for different purposes. Some
pumped the water out of the coalmines, others hauled coal
to the surface, and still others set rolling mills, stamping

45

machines, etc, in motion. Several of them were of older design, had a less pleasing appearance, and consumed much fuel, to which they did not pay much attention at the mines, nor did they need to do so.[4]

However, the engine at Clandower [Landore?] deserves special mention. It was built according to Boulton & Watt's latest patent, with the strength of 70 to 80 horses, and lifted the water out of a coal mine from a depth of 48 fathoms. The pumps had a diameter of 20 inches, and the stroke was between 8 and 9 feet. The normal speed was 12 to 13 strokes per minute; it could, however, in an emergency be taken up to 60. It was calculated that it moved overall 1,100 gallons, or almost 1,500 Swedish quarts of water in a minute, which amounts to between 80,000 and 90,000 quarts per hour.

The hard porcelain factory. This, which belongs to a Mr George Haynes of Swansea, and is situated near the town, deserves to be seen by tourists, partly on account of the size of its production, and partly on account of some special plant. Among the latter is a machine for elutriating the clay, which afterwards goes through a gauze sieve; a mill for grinding the flints which are used for glazing and sometimes for mixing into the porcelain mass itself; a masonry-lined sump into which the elutriated material is poured or run in the form of a thin pulp, and heated from underneath by coal, until it has attained a certain density, when it is taken out and formed into large lumps, which are laid out to half-dry, and afterwards worked by hand until the mass is sufficiently plastic for throwing and forming; a pressing machine for moulding handles for larger and smaller vessels, etc. In one of the workshops, where there was written in large letters over the door: 'No admittance here' (wherein, however, Mr Haynes does admit those people who are specially recommended to him), teacups, basins, plates, etc, are painted in complete imitation of the coarse blue Chinese porcelain. These paintings, which are previously engraved on copper and transferred on to fine printing paper with a mixture of red cobalt, are, while they are still damp, pasted on the half-fired porcelain, allowed to dry for an hour, washed off, and afterwards covered with glaze, whereupon they are finally put in the kilns and fired blue.

In a small neighbouring room trees, branches, or more correctly, a kind of dendrites, were painted on beer mugs and the like in an adroit manner. A practised worker could paint two to three such vessels in a minute. Mr Haynes had also attempted to make some finer goods, but the factory was actually equipped for hard porcelain, which is sold at good prices in America and several places abroad, so that in the year he cannot make as much as is ordered.

On 18 or 19 March we left Swansea, and took our way through the little town of Neath, five Swedish miles away. The district is here, towards the sea coast, rather low, but in the distance considerable mountains and heights could be seen, which rise more and more towards the boundaries of Brecknockshire.

Shortly before Neath, a large new copper works is passed, on the right near Neath Abbey at a little distance from the road. Although I had not in fact been introduced to the proprietor, I yet had the opportunity of inspecting the works, which appeared to me to be laid out upon the same plan as those at Swansea, only perhaps rather more spacious.

Not far from here lay, on the left-hand side of the road, an ironworks belonging to Mr Fox & Co of Cornwall. We had letters from Mr Lockwood to a Mr Gould, who lived here, and we were allowed quickly to go through the workshops; these consisted of a blast furnace, a founding furnace, and a large hearth, which was presumably used for the production of so-called 'fine metal' for a wrought-iron works erected for the purpose, or perhaps also for sale. All these hearths received their blast from a large cylinder blower, which was driven by a steam engine, and which had a regulator with a movable cover of 9 feet diameter. There was nothing special about the blast furnace, the shaft of which was 63 feet high, and which only produced 15 to 16 tons of pig-iron per week, except that the shaft was dug out and built into the side of a hill which encroached into the works. The ironstone was, by comparison with that of Merthyr Tydfil, poor, but it was said that production could here be pushed higher, if they did not primarily consider the quality of the iron. The coal had, after it had been converted to coke, almost the appearance of carbonised oak wood, and was said to be more free from sulphur than usual. Ironstone and coal were brought down from the hills above by railway. Besides the workshops mentioned, a turning shop had also been established, where, by means of a steam engine with the strength of three horses, rollers and various machine parts were turned.

On the other side of the town a new railway had been laid down to the harbour, also there was an alum works, which I was unable to see, since the proprietor had recently died. Anyway, I did not know of anything here which deserved special attention. We therefore took a post chaise to Pontneath Vaughan, a little place on the way to Brecknock, about two Swedish miles from Neath.

The country is here very hilly, and belongs to the coal district mentioned above; here and there, however, it is fairly well cultivated and somewhat wooded. The hills consist partly of the above-mentioned grey-black sandstone, which is used for building, and partly of several kinds of slate, above and below which coal and ironstone are encountered in several places. On the road, which here runs along the River Neath and the canal of the same name, we this freedom became all the more pleasant to us, because, from one of the high chalk mountains, which partially enclose, partly cut through and squeeze flat the coal seams, on one side we had a view to the sea through the beautiful valley in which the river Neath meanders, and on the other side we could see the surrounding mountains in Brecknock and Monmouthshire, whose rich treasures, like those of the English capitalists, do not glitter, but spend themselves unnoticed, and, in bare fields where a few years ago the wanderer could scarcely find shelter from the weather, have created great cities and fruitful meadows. The valley below at the foot of the above-mentioned chalk mountains was almost unpopulated and little cultivated, but farther on towards Merthyr we passed some railroads, and a great highway between the ironworks and Pontneath Vaughan, which is supposed to be finished next year. In the distance lay some blast furnaces, which were recognisable by the black smoke of their steam engines.

Merthyr Tydfil, which a few decades ago was an unimportant place, has in recent times, through its great ironworks, become one of the most remarkable places in England. These ironworks, which are known by four different names, Cyfarthfa, Pen-y-daren, Dowlais, and Plymouth, and belong to as many proprietors or companies, all lie together in an area scarcely half a Swedish mile long and a half a quarter-mile wide. In this little district one encounters thirteen blast furnaces in operation, which produce weekly something like 40 tons of pig-iron and castings, or over 180,000 shippounds annually. Besides that about 20,000 tons or 150,000 shippounds of wrought iron, hoop iron, bolt iron and sheets are prepared here annually. Without a knowledge of the situation of these works and the refining process now usual in England, the possibility of such a production is difficult to imagine. I will therefore give a short sketch of the locality and the smelting process, high, if they had not here adopted the so-called puddling process, which was invented about twenty years ago by an Englishman named Cort, afterwards tried out in several places in England, and had almost been abandoned again, when it was finally brought to perfection through the persistent efforts of Mr Crawshay at Cyfarthfa, so that during the last war between 70,000 and 80,000 shippounds of wrought iron were made, which is said to have yielded a pure profit of £50,000 sterling or more. This quite unique process, which has already been adopted for some years, albeit with various modifications, in the whole of England and at some works in Scotland and Ireland, has shared the common fate of some other large-scale chemical operations, in that it has been neither thoroughly known nor described. The only printed description which to my knowledge has so far appeared, is in the *Journal des Mines* for last year, and was by a young American, Mr Smith, who had seen the puddling work at the Ketteley [Ketley] ironworks of Mr Raynolds [Thomas P. Smith, 'Note sur la fabrication du fer et de l'acier avec la houille, d'après les procédés de M. William Reynoldt', *Journal des Mines*, 13 (An XI), 52-60]. However, this description shows, although it was originated by an otherwise skilled man, that the author certainly lacks practical knowledge of the manipulation of iron, without which one cannot correctly grasp and properly describe such an operation. Also Mr Smith's description gives only an incomplete idea of the process, which at Pen-y-daren is briefly as follows: After the raw iron has been tapped out of the blast furnace in the usual way and formed into cast pieces or pigs, weighing a few Swedish pounds, and approximately of the same shape as at the blast furnaces in Gästrikland, these are laid in the foundry sand to cool for an hour. From here the iron is taken to the so-called refinery, which consists of one or more hearths, almost the same as our refining forges, only larger and deeper. Here the pigs are broken into two or more pieces, partly in order to get them more easily into the hearth, and partly in case of necessity to arrange a suitable mixture of grey and white or soft and hard pig-iron. Usually 10 to 15 hundredweights, or 75 shippounds pig-iron weight of these pieces is put into such a hearth at once, and when, within two or three hours, it is completely melted down, the tapping out is done in exactly the same way as at the blast furnace. The material thus obtained, which is nothing other than a refined raw iron, is cast in sand into pigs such as have just been described; they are, however, not allowed to cool longer than is necessary for them to be picked up, whereupon water is poured over them, partly in order to wash the casting sand from the surface, and partly also to give the iron a certain hardness. Such a pig iron is called 'fine metal', is laminar and white in fracture, and more or less resembles the rather hard and not very red-short Dannemora pig-iron.

Now the so-called puddling process begins. The pigs just obtained are broken in several pieces, 3 to 4 hundredweights, or 15 to 20 shippounds pig-iron weight of which are taken to a specially built reverberatory furnace (puddling furnace). In this furnace the iron remains undisturbed for three-quarters of an hour, or as long as is necessary, until it is usually glowing right through, and is so loose on the surface that it can be broken up with a stirrer and brought in pieces to the floor of the furnace. The puddler carries on with this breaking and stirring until all the pieces have disappeared and have been dispersed in a thick gritty mass. This usually requires half an hour, and the iron—which has already taken on a lighter colour, as a sign that the refining has begun—often appears to boil, as in our German fire-refining process. In this period the puddler works, allows the mass to stand, increases or decreases the heat, now and then pours water into the furnace, each according to necessity and as is indicated by the phenomena of refining. After a few minutes the mass now takes on a more or less pasty appearance, becomes bright and tough, and can no longer be worked with the stirrer, but it must be broken up and divided into smaller pieces, which are worked backwards and forwards, divided anew once or several times, and afterwards collected together into a lump or as much as is necessary for an iron bar. Usually five, six, or up to seven such pieces or so-called lumps are made at each puddling, which, as quickly as is possible, are taken out of the furnace and brought under a large helve hammer, where they are shaped into the form of our hammered billets. These, which are now called blooms or balls, are again put into another reverberatory furnace, named a bloom- or ball-furnace, from where, after proper heating they are brought under the rolls and rolled out into bars at a single heat. At Pen-y-daren I saw bars 12 to 13 feet long, $2\frac{1}{2}$ inches wide, and $3/8$ inch thick rolled in half an hour, which could be continued as long as blooms were available. The rolled bars are certainly very even, but in order to get a still finer surface, freed from mill scale, they are subjected to yet another operation, which is called the 'smoothing process'. This merely consists of placing the bars in a heating furnace, and after a gentle heating, they are put under a cast-iron hammer, and with a few blows cleared of the mill scale which has already been loosened by the heating.

It is true that at Dowlais this process differs in some respects from that just described; however, the foregoing can suffice to give an idea of the English bar-forges, to the extent that is necessary to an understanding of what follows.

The number of workshops in all the ironworks is unknown to me, however, at Pen-y-daren alone there are three blast furnaces, three refineries, twenty-five puddling-

and eight bloom-furnaces, with the necessary hammers and rolling mills, as well as nine or ten steam engines, some of which act with the strength of 70 to 80 horses. These installations are, however, not adequate for the annual bar iron production of about 8,000 tons, but more raw iron and fine metal is obtained from two nearby blast furnaces, which are operated almost throughout the year for Mr Homfray's account. Little pig-iron or cast goods are sold from these works, but the requirement for buildings, rails, wheels, rolls, etc, is all the greater since everything which in our forges is usually made of wood, is here of cast iron. Besides the beams which carry the roof, the floor of the hammer mill and a long footway outside it are of cast iron, and I was assured that a pine beam of a certain strength cost more than a piece of cast iron which would be adequate for the same purpose. It is said that the number of workers in all the works runs to about 4,000, of which 900 are engaged at Pen-y-daren, reckoning in the miners. One can easily imagine how insignificant is this number, by comparison with that which might be necessary with us for such a great production.

Besides a number of smaller railways, on which coal and ironstone is brought to the blast furnaces, Mr Homfray has laid down a larger one for the transport of the bar iron, which runs for nearly seven Swedish quarter-miles close to the Cardiff Canal. On this railway two waggons coupled together and loaded with ten tons of bar iron are comfortably hauled by one horse, whose daily work consists of taking the iron from here to the loading point on the canal and afterwards bringing back the empty waggons. From Cyfarthfa directly opposite, a musket-shot from Pen-v-daren, the iron is loaded directly into boats of about 20 tons burthen, on the Cardiff Canal. When I expressed my astonishment that with such a situation of the canal they had still laid down a railway in the same direction, I was assured that the cost of this was fully recouped by the saving in lock dues and of time. It was added that the canal company loses just as little thereby, because, according to the company's patent, all profits from the canal in excess of 8 per cent are supposed to be devoted to a public institution in the town, and the canal now brings in between 7 and 9 per cent. This canal, which begins at Cyfarthfa goes down for 23 English miles or rather more to Cardiff, and has in this length 52 locks, 14 feet wide and 4 to 5 feet deep. The total drop is 530 feet, which, since it is almost equally divided among all the locks, makes about 10 feet for each. The lock dues are six pence per ton for every English mile, which, reckoning in the maintenance of the boats and other expenses, makes about twelve shillings and six pence per ton for the whole distance.

At these, as at most of the other ironworks in England, a tourist has the opportunity of admiring the strength and size of the engines which operate the blast bellows, hammers, and rolling mills. An English helve hammer weighs at least 60 to 70 shippounds, an axle-shaft 100 to 150 of the same; flywheels on rolling mills from 50 to 60 shipping pounds, etc. Some of them are cast in a single piece; however, besides these one finds assembled machines which weigh 200, 300, and up to 700 shippounds and more. Of the last-mentioned kind, however, I only know of one which is in operation, and one other which is being built. That which I met with in operation at Cyfarthfa, consisted of an overshot water wheel, 52 feet in diameter and 7 feet wide in the buckets. The whole thing, apart from the buckets, consisted of cast iron, and the shaft journals were over 12 inches in diameter. Certain parts of this wheel which were cast in one piece weighed more than 60 shippounds, and it is not unbelievable when one is told that the whole thing weighs more than 100 tons or 750 shippounds. A steam engine (with the strength of 70 to 80 horses) has been connected to this wheel by a kind of connecting rod, so that both machines in common operated the blast bellows for two blast furnaces and several refineries. When there is plenty of water much fuel can thereby be saved in the steam engine, and if there is a lack of water the works can be kept going by a stronger firing under the boiler. Concerning the usefulness of these combined machines people in England were of differing opinions. Some believed that Mr Crawshay had merely built such a thing as a kind of oddity to show what could be done; but I have reasons for believing that it really has its advantages, for otherwise they would not have decided to build a similar if not larger machine in one of the neighbouring works, which is managed by a very discerning foundryman. It is true that the power of the wheel and of the steam engine sometimes work against one another, or, more accurately, that part of the power of one of them, when it is running the faster, is lost in driving the one which is going slower. But thereby there results a more even movement than one can usually attain from a steam engine alone, in so far as it is not equipped with a special governor, which often detracts somewhat from the power. Besides that, the large overshot water wheel here acts as a flywheel, and maintains for a long time the motion which it has received from the increased speed of the steam engine. At Pen-y-daren there was such a combined machine on a smaller scale, with which they were very satisfied. Perhaps I shall on a future occasion have an opportunity of explaining this combination in more detail by means of a drawing; in the meantime it is easily comprehensible to those who know the usual transmission of several kinds of mechanical motion through steam engines.

Before I leave the works at Merthyr I must say something about a machine for stamping horseshoes, which was invented a short time ago and brought into operation at

Pen-y-daren. I already heard it spoken of in London as a great curiosity in iron manufacture, and I also saw samples of the horseshoes made with it, which were as fine and well made as the forged ones. It was feared that this machine would not only ruin a great number of shoeing smiths in London but would also substantially reduce the sales of Swedish bar iron. When I arrived at Merthyr the machine had already been taken to pieces, and some of the cog-wheels belonging to it had been used for the above-mentioned water- and steam-engine. It had been found that partly owing to the many dies for the diverse sizes and forms of horseshoes, partly on account of the expensive warehouses for promoting the sales, it cost too much to maintain, for the sales were insufficient in England to dispose of the large and rapid production.

Mr Greville had indeed recommended us to Mr Homfray, but the latter was now in London, and we therefore did not have the pleasure of making the personal acquaintance of this enlightened and patriotic ironmaster. He had, however, given orders before his departure that all the workshops should be open to us, so that we were able to inform ourselves about everything. A Mr Lyndon, who now had the principal oversight at Pen-y-daren, therefore sought to make up to us as far as possible for the loss of Mr Homfray's presence, and I must acknowledge that I have sometimes left ironworks with less satisfaction in my fatherland, where I ought to some extent to have received explanations as a matter of right.

In order better to survey the continuation of the remarkable stretch of country wherein most of the ironworks lie, we decided to make the journey from Merthyr to Abergavenny, about four Swedish miles, on foot. To this end Mr Lyndon gave us letters to two ironmasters, Fothergill and Monkhouse, who lived at the Sirhowy Ironworks, 5 or 6 quarter-miles from Merthyr, and who were just engaged in founding a new works, named Tredegar. At the works of Dowlais, which one passes before leaving Merthyr, were a great number of railways for the transport of ore and coal, as well as the delivery of iron and chalk to the canal. Higher up, the countryside took on a wild and desert appearance; the so-called roadway was almost unusable for wheeled vehicles; but all around on the slopes of the hills appeared railways, which crossed between the coal mines and several ironworks in the distance. About half way between Sirhowy and Merthyr we had a sight which caused us no little amazement. This was a number of mules, laden with coal and ironstone, which were in baskets hung over pack saddles; these animals took the materials half a mile or a mile to some blast furnace, or also to the nearby railways. In just the same manner I also saw raw iron castings transported from a blast furnace in the neighbourhood to the railway which ran to Dowlais. It was extraordinary, at a distance of half a Swedish mile from a place where such great resources are employed for the facilitation of the transport of goods, to see a reversion from the normal use of vehicles. However, they have either not yet arrived at the point of laying down railways here, or they had a mind to discontinue the work here, which is now carried on with inconsiderable profit, or perhaps at a loss. One mule is said to be able to carry three hundredweights or nearly sixteen Swedish pounds in the manner described; they were about the same size as Swedish farm horses.

Nearer to Sirhowy the railways became more general. On one of them fifteen little waggons coupled together were hauled by two quite moderately sized horses; however, we were told that on the best tramroads two such horses could pull nineteen such waggons, each loaded with 15 hundredweights, which makes more than 7 tons, or about 52 shippounds, for each horse.

Sirhowy has two blast furnaces and some refineries, the

production of which mostly goes down to the works at Merthyr, or is also shipped from the nearest harbour. At the moment they were here building up stocks of raw iron for the puddling furnaces and rolling mills being completed at Tredegar, which lies near to Sirhowy. These two works can, notwithstanding that they are under distinct ownership, be to some extent regarded as one in respect of the position and the people interested in them. Mr Fothergill and Mr Monkhouse, who were either shareholders in Sirhowy, or at any rate had the principal management of it, were also shareholders in the new works, and ran here a business of the highest class, in which otherwise Mr Homfray of Pen-y-daren and Mr Thomson & Co of London were the principal shareholders and retailers. In regard to situation and the arrival of materials these works were likewise not to be neglected by comparison with those at Merthyr. At Sirhowy a gallery came out of the mountain a few yards from the doors of the refinery; that this tunnel is not now used for coal and ore transport probably proves nothing more than that they have found an even less expensive way of bringing these materials to the blast furnace, where the coal is turned into coke and afterwards tipped or hoisted out.

At Tredegar, where already the foundations for a few score puddling furnaces had been laid and a new blast furnace with a double shaft was in full operation, the locality seems certainly at first glance to be less favourable, but when one considers the plant as a whole, one soon sees that this is an error. Probably this works, which was not thought of until three years ago, can in a short time become one of the principal, if not the premier works in England; at least, I could think of no new installation of ironworks which had been made with such a careful consideration of the sales and such prospects of mitigation of the running costs. They had already convinced them-the following day at this works, whose proprietors received us with unaffected courtesy, we continued on our way to Abergavenny. For my part I could not without sadness leave a place where there was still so much to see, and where the few hours' discussion with Messrs Fothergill and Monkhouse would certainly have been more useful to me than a stay of several days in another place. My travelling companion had, however, determined the time when he would have to be back in London; furthermore people were beginning to talk of war, and it was perhaps necessary to speed up the tour, if we were not to be obliged to alter our itinerary. All the same, my dissatisfaction increased, as on the way to Abergavenny I saw on either side several coal quarries and iron mines, a large number of chalk quarries and limekilns, as well as many small ironworks and canals, upon which I could now only cast a fleeting glance in passing, but to which I could have had the best introductions from Mr Fothergill. Besides that we left on our right, at a distance of a few miles, the tinplate- and japanning-works at Pontypool,[7] as well as several works and establishments which would probably have repaid closer acquaintance. The country, since we had left Merthyr, had shown the same monotonous aspect as that between the latter place and Pontneath Vaughan, until we were some miles behind Sirhowy, where the slate and chalk hills, especially in the neighbourhood of a little river, were steeper and more rugged, and at the same time cut through by water. Right across the river ran a canal on an aqueduct almost 50 feet high and with an arch so large that the river could continue to flow unhindered beneath it. Neither my guidebook nor my maps could give me the slightest information about this river and canal, as was the case with many other objects of this district. My curiosity would, indeed, certainly have been satisfied by a map of the waterways, canals, and railways of South Wales, which I saw at Mr

Fothergill's, but it had, as I afterwards heard from Mr Carry, who had had it engraved, not been published for sale, but for a special purpose. The nearer we came to Abergavenny, the more the countryside lost its wild appearance, and the difference in the climate upon descending the mountains rather more than a quarter of a mile from the town was considerable. On the slopes of the hills several fields were green, and some shrubs and trees were in full bloom.

According to Mr Greville's programme we should now have gone direct to Hereford, about 3½ Swedish miles from Abergavenny. We should then have had to pass a high region where there are neither quarries nor mines, but which has a certain value for a mineralogist. However, our innkeeper, who was more concerned about his horses than about all the observations which we were to make there, in which perhaps he may not have been altogether wrong, represented the way to us as being so difficult that even with four horses in front of a post-chaise we should not have covered even half the distance before nightfall. We therefore took a post-chaise to Monmouth, where we stayed overnight. On this journey we saw a beautiful district, admirably cultivated, wooded here and there with deciduous timber, and dotted with clean farmhouses and fine country estates.

On the following morning we continued our journey through the towns of Hereford, Leominster, and Ludlow to Bridgnorth, about 10½ Swedish miles. On this road the district is more uneven than level, and at some little distance heights could be seen, which, to judge from their form, have much similarity to the Kinnekulle. On the streets around Hereford houses were made of a kind of stone which resembles fairly closely the coarse-grained basalt of the stratified mountains of West Gotland. Farther on there was limestone, which likewise may have been brought down from the surrounding hills. These heights, which are most considerable north-west of Bridgnorth or north of Ludlow, have the name 'Morvan Hills' [This must be a reference to the 'Malvern Hills', but Svedenstierna has misplaced them, for they are 30-40 miles south of where he indicates], and seem to be set upon the still higher primeval mountains of north Wales, which here stretch out towards the shore of the Severn. The towns and country houses are here, as in Monmouthshire, mostly built of brick, and certainly give to the district a more pleasing appearance than the heavy black-grey or white-painted houses of squared stone in Wales. The country is also on the whole fairly cultivated, but one sees nothing of factories or ironworks except at Bridgnorth, where we arrived in darkness, and saw from a hill before the town the glow of the furnaces of several foundries and glassworks which are established on the banks of the Severn above and below the town. About halfway to Broseley, or scarcely half a Swedish mile from there, one begins to notice already the proximity of the coal seams. Still nearer to Broseley and Coalbrookdale a great number of horse-whims and chimneys are to be seen at the mines, the number of which increases, the nearer one gets to the last-named place.

as the iron bridge, which was the first of its kind in England, have made this place so well known abroad. Although the mass of houses, buildings, works, etc, situated here, appear to a traveller as a coherent town, the whole is here nevertheless divided into Broseley, Ironbridge, and Coalbrookdale. Under the latter name is actually understood the valley itself, which comes out northwards above the iron bridge, and wherein lie several ironworks under the names of 'Dale Works' or 'Dale Company Works'.

Close to Broseley, on the above-mentioned level ground down to the Severn, lies the Calcutt Ironworks, owned by a Mr Brodie, of London. It consists of three blast furnaces, a few remelting or so-called air-furnaces, a cannon-boring machine and turning shop, as well as several workshops connected with the foundry. The blast furnaces, of which two were in operation, and one was being overhauled, are not so large as those in South Wales, and, like the other local furnaces, seldom give more than thirty or so tons of iron in a week, whereas the Welsh ones are driven up to fifty tons or more weekly. The pig-iron is here certainly better and more serviceable for fine and strong castings. A Mr Brodie (a relative of the proprietor) declared that the cannon cast here exceeded in strength those which had formerly been made in Cumberland or Lancashire with charcoal, and I can doubt this all the less since, among the other cast wares which Mr Brodie showed us were some iron rails, 2 inches wide, $\frac{1}{2}$ inch thick and 8 feet long, under one end of which an eight- or nine-inch high support was placed, while the other end rested on the ground, and upon which we could stand. In this manner we tested several rails, backwards and forwards, without their either breaking or bending. Rails of this kind are used instead of bar iron as supports at small openings in walls, and for setting into fire-hearths, or so-called stoves, where they certainly give the same service as wrought iron. Here, as everywhere else in England, the casting is merely in sand, and that from the smallest pieces of less than one ounce weight to a weight of 8 to 9 tons, as well as cannon of every calibre. Mr Brodie confirmed from his experience something which I had always believed, namely that just as good cannon could be cast directly from the blast furnace as from a reverberatory furnace or air furnace, if only the charge and the blast are adapted accordingly.

The boring of the cannon is here done by means of a steam engine, which acts directly on a crank fixed in the centre of a shaft, from which eleven horizontal borers are in turn driven through gearing. Mr Brodie did indeed say that our boring method, where the borer revolves with the cannon vertical, could have certain advantages where the output is only small; here, however, where sometimes orders of 5,000 tons and more must be completed in a short time, it was necessary to bore and turn several at once.

At this works they had made attachments to the twenty furnaces according to Lord Dundonald's invention, in order to collect the bituminous parts of the coal when it is turned into coke. Since the furnaces and the tar obtained therein, are already described in the *Repertory of Arts and Manufactures* and in O'Reilly's *Journal des Arts et Manufactures*, I can be brief here. The ovens are vaulted with bricks and have, from inside and outside the appearance of a hayrick or a beehive of 7 to 8 feet height and diameter. In the side of the oven is an opening, through which the coal is loaded, and in the floor is a rectangular opening with strong and closely spaced firebars, below which is an ashpit with a hole in the outer wall. In the oven vault itself there is another opening, into which is fitted a cast-iron pipe of a few inches diameter, which leads into a brick-lined water reservoir. When the oven is filled, it is lit through the ash hole, and the large opening is, as soon as the coal is properly alight, bricked up. The smoke then goes out through the pipe in the roof and is condensed in the water container. In the process a quantity of hydrogen gas or inflammable air is evolved, which is led away from the reservoir through another pipe; the tar is tapped from the reservoir into a large basin, where it remains standing, in order to precipitate the impurities, and to separate most of the water away from it. This tar is, however, still unsuitable for most purposes, and must therefore undergo a kind of distillation, during which there comes over, mixed with some water, a strong empyroform oil, which has some similarity to our pitch oil. This oil is used for painting certain parts of buildings, and mixed with lampblack, for colouring fences and the like. The refined tar so obtained is either used like other tar, or it is also boiled down into pitch. They seem here to be satisfied with this installation, but it has been asserted that this tar, admittedly very useful for certain purposes, is detrimental to rigging, and that on the whole the invention has few advantages.[8]

Near to Calcutt lay some refineries and casting furnaces, but I do not know to whom they belong, and what is made there.

The so-called Dale Works have their beginning close by the entrance to Coalbrookdale, and then go on up the valley to an ironworks named Orsay [Horsehay], which likewise belongs to the Dale Company. The last named works has a better appearance, and seems to have been built later than the others. It consists of two blast furnaces, some refineries, puddling furnaces, and rolling mills. At the works lying further down are merely two blast furnaces and a few remelting furnaces, besides grinding machines and lathes. Here they make a quantity of fine castings, such as firegrates, weights, flatirons, stoves, screws for cider presses, and the like, which articles are mostly cast from reverberatory or also from so-called cupola furnaces, wherein small ingots and all kinds of broken scrap are melted down with normal blast. These cupola furnaces are only a few feet high and square, clad on the outside with cast-iron plates and on the inside with refractory bricks. The tuyère is very small, and often has a diameter of not more than an inch. The blast for such a furnace is either taken from the reservoir of the large blowing machine, or the furnace is itself provided with a small cylinder blower, which is worked by horses. Furnaces of this kind can be seen even in London, and in practically every foundry in the country, as described and illustrated in the *Repertory*, only they must not be confused with Wilkinson's small blast furnaces, in which the ore is smelted directly. All the blast furnaces and rolling mills at the Dale Works are driven by the usual large steam engines, but the lathes and grinding machines are operated by the water of a little brook, which winds down the length of the valley. Below the last-mentioned works, near to the Ironbridge, was a machine for boring cylindrical blowers, and a helve hammer, built quite in our fashion, which were both driven by water. The framework of the hammer was mostly of timber, but the hammer head, the water wheel, and the hammer stock were of cast iron. When the smith was to show me how drawing-down was done under such a hammer, which at present are very rare in England, he pulled out the gag too early, so that the hammer made seven or eight blows on the bare anvil, before the piece of iron came under it. I had no thought but that hammer and anvil would thereby be ruined, but the smith assured me that this was of no consequence, and that such a thing was very usual. I mention this in advance as a proof of how they here understand the art of giving the cast iron any desired property, and I shall hereafter, where this matter will be dealt with, seek to indicate the origins of such strength and toughness in certain kinds of cast iron. Several hearths and furnaces were attached to

attention of a traveller, is the iron bridge. I am afraid that
I no longer remember the length of the arch,[9] which is
anyway fully described in several places; however, I must
mention one circumstance, which bears witness to the
strength of such bridges. Some time earlier, before I came
there, the ground at one end had yielded, and yet people
drove over the bridge without noticing it, until some bolts
had either broken or bent, and it was clearly seen, that
certain parts of the structure began to separate. These
parts were screwed together, the arch was tightened up as
well as possible, and meanwhile the displaced abutment
was strengthened, without the bridge having once been
unusable on this account. This iron bridge is otherwise
less remarkable in respect of its size and appearance, as
several finer and larger ones have since been built in England; however, it was the first of its kind, and served to
prove the usefulness of such bridges, of which the majority
of people are now so far convinced that Parliament has
agreed to an iron bridge over the Thames, in place of
London Bridge, which is partly beginning to sink and
which greatly obstructs shipping on the river. The last-
mentioned bridge is 915 feet long and 45 feet wide, which
may also be exactly the dimensions of the projected arch
for the new iron bridge.

Beside the old iron bridge at Coalbrookdale, two others
have recently been built over the Severn, one above Broseley, and the other below Ironbridge, in the middle of the
village of Little Wenlock. The latter has a much lighter
and more pleasing appearance than the old bridge.[10]

At all the ironworks, as well as at the coalmines, there
are a great many large and small railways, which are sometimes 1 to 2 English miles long.

The ironstone occurs here partly in the same manner as
at the ironworks in Wales, in horizontal deposits a few
inches thick above or below the coal seams, partly in the

form of flattened spheres in a semi-hard shale, likewise lying within the coal seams. In order not to repeat the description of the ironstone, I remark here once for all, that such, in England as well as in Scotland, is entirely of one single kind, and belongs to the so-called stratified ores;[11] it may, however, occur in deposits or in the form of balls. It is, it is true, sometimes variable in content, mixed with more or less pyrites, but generally has the same behaviour in the smelting process. The red, occasionally spherical and shining haematite from Cumberland and Lancashire is smelted at but few blast furnaces and in tiny quantities; it is seldom found outside the districts mentioned.

The coal seams here lie near the surface; they are more irregular, and have a greater dip than those in South Wales, and are usually of greater thickness. The hauling is done by means of horse-whims or small steam engines, and the shafts are seldom over 8 to 10 fathoms, sometimes not more than 5 fathoms deep. The method of working is quite simple: first of all the coal is taken out within a certain part of the area and afterwards as much ironstone as is required, after which the mine is abandoned. Everywhere in this district collapsed shafts and depressions in the earth can be encountered, even where there are houses and gardens. Some houses were in fact broken down, or stood so slantwise, that I could not conceive how anyone could live in one of them.

A bare Swedish half-mile from Ironbridge, on the left of the way to Shifnall [Shifnal], lies the ironworks of Lightmoor, the head of which is a Mr Homfray, brother of the Mr Homfray at Pen-y-daren. It consists of three blast furnaces, some refineries and bloom- or ball-furnaces. Most of the pig-iron is here cast into pigs, from which 'fine metal' and material iron is made, which is sent to Worcestershire, in order to be worked up into sheets, bars, nail-rods, etc at some of the works belonging to the Lightmoor company. Some pig-iron is also used for casting, partly direct from the blast furnaces, partly after it has undergone a new melting in a reverberatory furnace. The process here was very different from that in use at Merthyr. Here also the principal purpose was to make good iron, and they had been so fortunate in this that the iron from Lightmoor was sold at the same price as our average kinds. Mr Ton, who managed this works, affirmed that no bars sold for less than £23 sterling per ton, and that up to £26 sterling was paid for the larger pieces, for steam engines, etc. Mr Boulton junior, of Soho [Birmingham], afterwards told me that there they often use the Lightmoor iron instead of the best Swedish, not because it was in general better, but because, when one orders good iron from Lightmoor, one most certainly gets good iron; however, if one buys from the best Swedish brands, one occasionally finds among it bars, or what is still worse, certain parts of bars, which are badly worked. I often heard this complaint about our Swedish iron in England, and personal observation also showed me that it was well founded; but I should not fail to mention that certain brands were quite free from this complaint, that others had been improved, and that if a smith has to do some really good work, he prefers to take Swedish iron for it. At Lightmoor, moreover, they certainly had less profit from the wrought iron which was sold there for £23 sterling and more, than the Merthyr works did from theirs at £17 to £18. But the English are often satisfied with small profits, in order to get definite sales, while on the other hand manufacturers in other lands are often obliged to calculate differently.

The three blast furnaces and a few refineries were served by a single steam engine with a power of 90 or so horses. The cylinder blower was 7 feet 4 inches internal diameter, 5 feet stroke; it had two regulators of the same size, with movable covers, from where the blast was divided. Each cover was weighted with 10 tons of iron, and the hiss of the blast from the tuyère was so strong that one could not hear a word spoken. In order to give a brief idea of the friction in such an engine, I may remark that the beam, which here consisted of two oaken beams, bound with iron bands, and which was in total about 18 feet long, $2\frac{1}{4}$ feet deep, and $1\frac{1}{2}$ feet wide, had loosened itself on its axis to such an extent, when the engine was finished, that they were induced to patch it in the middle with a strong plate of cast iron. This engine was quite new, and built according to the last patent of Messrs Boulton & Watt. It went so quietly and easily, if I except the hissing of the blast and the noise of the valves, that a badly made spinning wheel often causes more noise.

Round about Lightmoor were railways, some laid down by the nearby mines, some by the Shropshire Canal, where at the loading place small waggons with limestone were let down over an inclined plane. This limestone came from a distance of a few miles in barges of 8 tons burthen, which, however, could now only be loaded with 5 tons on account of lack of water. Several such barges were coupled behind one another, and a horse could in this manner pull 100 tons and more.

At one mine, where the haulage was done by means of a steam engine, and the rope was wound over a horizontal axle, they are now using a kind of flat rope, about 3 inches wide and a finger thick. This rope, which is described in O'Reilly's *Journal des Arts et Manufactures*, is, as it were, plaited, and the fabric is not unlike the plaited watch-guards. They had been trying these ropes for too short a time to be able to judge of their advantages over other ropes in respect of durability, otherwise, they behaved the same as ordinary ropes.

After a stay of some days in Coalbrookdale and Broseley,

we continued our journey to Birmingham, through Shifnal,
Wolverhampton, and Wednesbury. On the way to Shifnal,
which lies about a Swedish mile from Ironbridge, we
passed three large ironworks; Orsay [Horsehay], which has
already been mentioned earlier; Ketteley [Ketley], which
belongs to Mr Raynolds, and another small but newly built
works, whose owner is not known to me. I should very
much like to have seen Ketteley [Ketley], partly because
the American, Smith [Thomas P. Smith, of Philadelphia]
mentioned earlier, had there collected the material for his
description of the puddling process, and partly because Mr
Raynolds had set up several large-scale experiments, to
make steel with an addition of manganese. However, if in
England one has no special letter of introduction, and
particularly if one, as a stranger, presents oneself in the
company of a Frenchman, one can expect nothing better
than what now happened to us: Mr Raynolds very politely
regretted the fact that we were not provided with letters
of introduction, and that he was therefore obliged to refuse
us a courtesy which he otherwise gladly extends to strangers. I found this answer so correct, that I could not press
any further to see the works; however, I received permission to inspect an inclined plane in Mr Raynolds's garden,
over which boats were let up and down to a canal lying
below. It is true that these inclined planes are illustrated
and described in the *Repertory* or in Foulton's works
[Robert Fulton, *A Treatise on the Improvement of Canal
Navigation* (London, 1796)], but a short description of this
one may not be out of place here.

The water level of the upper canal was, to judge by eye,
36 to 40 feet above that of the lower one. At the end of the
upper canal were two locks side by side, each of which had
its gate above and a sluice below, which could be wound
up by means of a chain lying over a horizontal axle. Inside
these two locks the ground sloped, and was connected with

a plane, which ran down to the lower canal at an angle of 35 to 40 degrees. This plane, which, like the locks was double, on account of up- and down-going boats, was laid with iron rails, just like a railway. Centrally above the two locks was a horizontal axle with double ropes, and at each end of the axle was fixed a strong drum, of twice, if not three times the diameter of the shaft. Over these drums were strong brakes, which could be held on through a lever by a single man, so that the drum instantly came to a stop from full revolutions.

The boats used for navigating this canal were strongly built, about $6\frac{1}{2}$ feet broad, 2 feet deep and 16 yards long, and equipped with four cast-iron wheels, half the diameter of which extended into the bottom of the boat, the other half being outside, so that the axles could run in metal boxes which were fastened beneath the bottom of the boat. The forward wheels were nearly $1\frac{1}{2}$ feet and the rear ones barely 1 foot high, in order to maintain the boats properly in a horizontal position, as is also usual on inclined planes for waggons. Such a boat could carry eight tons or sixty shippounds; they were, however, on account of lack of water, only laden with five tons.

Now, when a loaded boat was to go down the incline, one lock was filled with water from the upper canal, and the boat was pulled into it. The gate was thereupon closed and the water was let out through a small opening in the above-mentioned sluice. A strong gallows three to four feet high was set up centrally above the boat, the vertical members being inserted into strong sockets on the outer sides of the boat. In the centre of the crossbeam which connected the two uprights, a rope was fastened, the other end of which was fastened to the bows of the boat. A further double rope went to each corner of the gallows, and was attached to the rope lying over the shaft. At the lower canal lay an empty boat, which was fastened in the same manner to the rope running down, and when all this had been done, the sluice at the lower end of the lock was wound up. The boat, which had already taken up its slanting position, and the wheels of which ran on the railway mentioned, now began to run down through its own weight, and at the same time pulled up the empty boat. In order to moderate the running, the brakes were put on, and when the empty boat reached the other lock, the lower sluice was closed, the lock filled, the upper gate opened, and the boat now went out into the upper canal. The man who directed the work said that if they wanted to operate at highest capacity, twenty-four pulls could be made in the hour.

As soon as we were past Shifnal, the district up to Wolverhampton became more and more flat. Between these two towns, over a distance of two or three Swedish miles, there were no mines, but the countryside had an admirable appearance, and seemed, like that which we had travelled through, to be very well cultivated. Towns and country houses here are mostly of brick, and built in the usual English style.

From Wolverhampton, where we arrived in good time in the afternoon, we immediately made an excursion to the nearby ironworks. These are generally laid out on a smaller scale than those described up till now, but their numbers are all the greater. The production is also here more divided, so that some ironmasters simply have blast furnaces, others foundries, and still others puddling- and rolling mills. The blast furnaces seemed to me almost smaller than at Coalbrookdale; they were all built of brick and with long charging bridges, like ours. At one of these blast furnaces, where we spent some time, the ironstone and coal was brought up the loading bridge by a small horse-whim, which was not dissimilar to the little ones usual at our mines, but better made. At one works, named Bilston New

G

Mills, and owned by a Mr Pearson and Company, I saw a puddling process which was different in certain details from that in South Wales. A kind of rough material iron was made here, which was cut up into nail-rods in a normal slitting mill with eight discs, so that from each bar an equal number of rods, about 5/16 inch square, was obtained.

Sometimes these nail-rods were cut from bars which were rolled directly from the lumps or blooms and at the same heat; sometimes also they were cut from bars which were annealed in specially built furnaces, and which had gained in quality through a rather more extended process.

As, late in the evening, we returned to Wolverhampton, which is only a quarter of a mile away, we saw the glow of fires from a great number of works in the remarkable plain between Wolverhampton, Wednesbury, Birmingham, and Dudley, about which I shall soon have several things to say.

The following day the journey went on to Birmingham, which is so famed on account of its factories, and on account of the vast quantity of ornamental and metal wares which for thirty years have been distributed from there all over the world. The town has a fine situation in the centre of a rich and cultivated district. Its regular parks, fine buildings, many and large factories; all these taken together with the splendid fields and canals, which latter partly surround the town, partly run through it, make it one of the most interesting towns in the world. Through these canals communication has been opened in recent times between Birmingham and the four principal trading towns and seaports in the kingdom, namely, London, Liverpool, Hull, and Bristol. If one takes into account that the population has decreased since the political upheavals at the beginning of the French Revolution, it may still with certainty be reckoned at nearly 60,000 souls. Certain manufacturing concerns, whose products merely depend upon the moods of fashion, are certainly in decline, and other rising towns have perhaps in recent years shared the profits with Birmingham. But all this cannot be noticed by a tourist, to whom objects of admiration present themselves at every step, and who only sees the plain evidence of riches and industry. Anyone who wishes to acquire precise knowledge of the town and its buildings, canals, etc, will find some good information about it in Huttons's description, which at the same time is so poor in notes about factories and manufactures, like all other descriptions of towns and provinces in England.

My travelling companion had letters from M. Prony in Paris to the famous Watt, who, in partnership with Mr Boulton, has not only brought the steam engine to its present perfection, but has also worked out a large number of mechanical inventions at the great Soho works, near Birmingham. This factory, which Boulton and Watt have now given over to their sons, in order to enjoy in tranquillity the fruits of many years of work, is closed to all strangers without exception. We knew this already from the notices which, on account of the constant flow of tourists, they had had inserted in the newspapers, and we therefore presented our letters merely with the intention of obtaining from Mr Watt some general information about the town, and those things which deserved our special attention there. This desire was, so far as the shortness of the time allowed, fulfilled, and his son, James Watt, also had the kindness to suggest on the following day an excursion to Dudley and the district thereabouts, upon which he would accompany us.

We therefore met Mr J. Watt the following morning on his estate, a distance from Soho, and thus took the road direct to Dudley Castle, which is now quite in ruins, but the situation of which on one of the heights which enclose the above-mentioned plain between Wolverhampton and

79

Birmingham, makes the place very notable for anyone who wishes to obtain an idea of the surrounding district. One sees from here several towns, and a great number of iron-works and factories, coalmines, limekilns, etc, and at the same time by coincidence looks out over the most splendid fields that one can imagine, which are everywhere traversed by canals and highways, and settled with pleasant houses and magnificent estates, scattered in beautiful groupings.

In the last-mentioned plain, which extends north and south for a mile and a quarter to a mile and a half between Dudley Castle and Wolverhampton, and about the same distance to the east and west, one can count 39 or 40 large and small ironworks, of which some merely produce pig-iron, others only bar iron, nail-rods, and the like. At some, it is true, one finds all these united at a single place, as at Browley [Rowley?], where the output of castings, bar iron, sheets, and cut iron is said to have amounted to about 6,000 tons in certain years. It is impossible to judge the total output of the works here, and just as impossible to get any reliable information about it. However, I believe I am not far out if I estimate the annual production of these works in wrought iron, counting in material of every kind, at at least 10,000 to 12,000 tons, or 90,000 shippounds. The production of pig-iron is still more difficult to calculate, especially since I do not know the number of blast furnaces exactly, but to judge from the pig-iron which one sees being transported on the canals to Birmingham and other places where there are foundries, it must indeed be considerable. All these works obtain their coal and ironstone from the coal seams lying in the above-mentioned plain, which are worked in just the same way as those at Coalbrookdale. I could not decide to what extent these seams were connected with those in Shropshire, but according to what the people here say about them they are separated from the latter by the chalk hills which surround the plain, and which are supposed to form a valley, 11 to 12 English miles long and 8 to 9 miles wide, under the earth, wherein the seams are laid down at a gradient of a few degrees towards a certain central point. Several seams one above the other and of unequal thickness are encountered here. The least thick, which are being worked, are from 9 to 14 feet, and lie the highest, often not more than 5 fathoms below the surface. Beneath these one meets at unequal depths, as one approaches the centre of the valley mentioned, another 30 to 40 feet thick coal seam, which at one place is already being worked 50 fathoms below the surface. The coal from this seam is, however, not so good as that from the thinner ones, but is sometimes mixed with a shaly clay and coal of lower quality. Not only are all the ironworks here supplied with coal and ore from these deposits, but there are also a great number of lime-kilns and other installations, which require much fuel, dependent upon them, not counting that which goes to Birmingham, Wednesbury, Wolverhampton, and several surrounding towns. On the Birmingham Canal alone the annual coal transport is reckoned at 8,000 or 9,000 tons per week, which at a rate of two shillings per ton or a little more, yields a revenue of about £1,000 per week. Through this canal, which is built for boats of 20 tons burthen, there therefore comes in annually over £50,000 sterling for coal, which almost amounts to the entire cost of building the canal and locks near Trollhätta in Sweden. Also the people with interests in this canal in Birmingham have had a good return on the capital which they advanced: for the shares, which at the completion of the canal stood at £140, rose in one year up to £1,150; afterwards they fell again to £800 and thereabouts, which is their present price.[12]

Immediately below Dudley Castle there are some large

quarries in the above-mentioned hills which cut through or enclose the coal seams. In one of these hills, which is undermined like a mine, there is a blasted-out canal several hundred yards long, which is linked to the canals outside in the fields. Here the boats go into the mountain, take on their loads and bring the limestone to the limekilns on the banks of the canal.

A few English miles from here, near the town of Wednesbury, lies the Bradley ironworks, belonging to Mr John Wilkinson. This is the largest in the whole district, and consists of two or three blast furnaces, various re-melting, puddling, and ball-furnaces, rolling mills for bar iron and sheets, and shearing mills as well as several other installations and workshops. It is asserted that in certain weeks nearly 200 tons of sheets, hoop-iron, bars, and nail-rods were made here. The last-named were sold to the people in the town, who work them by hand, particularly when there is no other work.

The smelting of the raw iron and the puddling process are said to be organised here in just the same way as at Bilston New Mills, but the rolling of the hot pieces obtained from the puddling furnaces was done in their own way, invented by Wilkinson himself. The rolling mill, driven by a steam engine, consisted of two five-feet diameter and six-feet long rolls, each of which consequently had a weight of 10 tons. Perhaps this is assuming too much, but I could estimate the weight of each roll at certainly 7 or 8 tons. At one end of this rolling mill were, as usual, grooved edges, and at the other, a smooth track. In the centre of the upper roll was a three-feet-long crank, which was connected to a strong rod standing vertically and fastened above to the beam of the steam engine, so that when the latter was in operation, the rod went up and down, but with such a small stroke that the crank could not make a complete revolution as usual, but went backwards and forwards within an angle of ninety degrees or more; the rolls acted therefore with merely a quarter of their periphery, instead of revolving completely. From the upper roll, which here acted simply by its own weight, there was no connection to the lower one, but this was merely driven by friction. When the first hot piece to be fed in had gone forwards and backwards four or five times, it was brought into the smooth track, and in the meantime a fresh piece was fed into the other end of the rolls, so that every time two heated pieces were drawn out at once. Wilkinson had believed that much time would thereby be saved, and he could actually use more puddling furnaces for this pair of rolls than for normal ones, but when one takes into account the cost of the original installation, the powerful movement in this machinery, and several inconveniences, it is not surprising that it has not been put to work anywhere else than in the inventor's works. The bars rolled here are rough at the edges, uneven, and on the whole badly worked. They must therefore go through a further process, before they are usable for sheets and ordinary bar iron.

The sheet mill consisted here of two or three furnaces and two pairs of rolls. The former resemble exactly the Swedish ones, only with the difference that in the floor forward by the furnace mouth were two holes five or six inches square, through which the flame shot out. Now, since the furnace stood cold, a couple of large coals were laid over these holes presumably to block the draught and at the same time to prevent cooling off. The rolls had a diameter of 10 to 12 inches and were three to four feet long, and were turned and polished. After the sheet iron had received a certain thinness in the rolls, two and two, and finally four and more were laid together. Some of the sheets made here were unusually large; larger than they are made in Sweden.

On the canal close to the works lay several barges of 20 tons, built from iron plates, and of just the same form as the ordinary wooden barges, that is to say, flat bottomed, blunt at the stern and triangular forward. In general they lay higher in the water and glided more easily than the wooden ones, remained fairly watertight, and withstood powerful blows, but cost three to four times as much as a wooden barge, and since one of the latter, with some maintenance, can be used for 20 years, it is still undecided how this experiment will pay. Wilkinson is said also to have built a larger vessel of iron plates on the Severn, which, however—I do not know why—has turned out less happily. He was at the time in London, and I was therefore not able to make his acquaintance personally, whereby I lost the opportunity of learning something about his experiments and installations. He is now an old man, but rich in new ideas, with which, however, he is said to have enriched science more than himself.

Near to Bradley a coal seam had been burning for several years, and gradually extended all round, so that over an area of a few hundred yards square, one sees smoke arising from the ground here and there. This seam, which lay only a few feet under the surface, had now been cut right through three to four fathoms deep, and one could therefore observe the action of this fire from the bottom to the surface, so far as the fire had taken hold. At the top there was a grey-white ash, presumably from the clayey surface soil, and where this had been blown or washed away, one saw cinder-like masses with holes and cracks through which the smoke ascended, the edges of which were encrusted with sulphur. Farther down, and in the part of the seam which had now cooled down, there was slag from the various substances which lay either in the coal itself or above and below it; the latter was in part completely burnt or turned into coke. The iron ore was partly roasted, partly sintered, and a part of the shale was transformed into a kind of porcelain, which was not dissimilar to the Wernish, but rather more glazed and slaggy. It was said that various small articles, such as buttons and the like, were carved from it. The other substances occurring in this seam bore, like those mentioned, greater or smaller marks of the action of the fire according to their unequal melting points and the distance from the places at which the fire was most concentrated. The above-mentioned cutting has been made in order to dig out grit and rubble for the roads in the neighbourhood, for which these semi-volcanic products had been found to be very serviceable.

Between Dudley Castle and Bradley one passes a place, which belongs to a Mr Keir, where various chemical operations are carried out on a large scale, such as the decomposition of common salt to soda, calcining of lead to minium, etc. We afterwards visited this Mr Keir, who is a skilled chemist; but partly we had no time, and partly also I did not believe that the owner would welcome it, if someone wanted to see the works.

On the way to Wednesbury, and right into the town, there were many coalmines, at which the haulage was done with small horse-whims, just as at the smaller iron mines in the mountain districts of Sweden. In Wednesbury and its neighbourhood, we saw several crooked and collapsed houses, as well as subsidences in fields, from the worked-out chalk seams, but these subsidences were scarcely noticeable, because they were nearly always covered with grass, or sown with corn and vegetables.

Mr James Watt, with whom we afterwards spent the evening, had a rather pleasing collection of minerals, with which he, without making any claim to the title of mineralogist, was very well acquainted. I found in this collection a series of coals from the mines in Scotland, which showed the gradations from the coal, in which the annual rings and branches could still be seen, to coke or carbonised coal. I also saw here some of the products which Faujas de St Fond, in his tour through Scotland, took to be volcanic, but which are merely fragments of the fortifications of the Picts, which were usually built of a type of stone similar to hornblende; these were brought to a half-melted state in the walls themselves by means of large wood fires, and in this manner formed layer by layer into a cohesive mass.

In his garden at Soho Mr Watt had set up a large example of the hydraulic ram of Montgolfier, from which the water, partly through pipes, partly with a hose, was conducted up a small eminence, and from here distributed in various directions.[13]

Before I left Birmingham, I inspected several of the canals mentioned earlier, which are all according to the same plan, with locks seven to eight feet wide, fifty to sixty feet long, and three, four, and up to five feet deep, partly walled with brick, and partly with dressed stone. The canals are either open ditches with sloping sides, or walled vertically with bricks, like the Dutch ones. Those which run through the town are sometimes culverted with bricks over a distance of several hundred yards, and streets run over these culverts, or houses are built on them. One of the canals, some distance from the town, crosses over a fairly large brook by means of an aqueduct. They are all provided with wide and comfortable towpaths, either on one side or on both sides.

It is easy to imagine what an enormous quantity of bricks is requisite for these installations, as well as for the town and the factories therein; but the manufacture of these is also as easy as can be. A kind of clay is found, especially at the end of the town, which is already mixed by nature with the proportion of sand necessary for good bricks, and no further effort is needed beyond digging out the clay and running on to it either rainwater or the water which trickles down from a small hill. When the clay has thereby become so soft that it can easily be worked, it is stirred up with a spade, and is then ready for moulding. Only invalids, women, and children were engaged in the work, and a sixteen-year-old girl asserted that she, with the help of another girl who brought the clay, and a small boy who carried away the bricks, could mould 3,000 ordinary building bricks in a day.

M. Bonnard's and my plan was actually to go from here by way of Lichfield, Stone, and Newcastle-under-Lyme, in the neighbourhood of which lies the famous Wedgwood Etruria porcelain factory, and from there to Leek, in order to visit some copper and lead mines belonging to the Duke of Devonshire, nearby at Eaton. However, my travelling companion, whose affairs hastened his return to France, was obliged to go direct to London immediately, and we therefore parted in Birmingham in the middle of April, after we had made the above-described tour of 800 to 900 English miles in five to six weeks together. I should be doing M. Bonnard an injustice if I did not acknowledge that his company was very valuable to me, and that I missed it with sadness. It is obvious that two, who travel for the same purpose, must see more than one, and that the opportunity to share our observations on the post coach, and to discuss certain matters, was advantageous for both of us. Also the costs of the journey for both of us were considerably reduced.

There is certainly no country where a traveller can in general enjoy every comfort of life with less obstruction and without further question; but just so there are few lands where a more careful eye is kept upon those who direct their attention to factories and mechanical installations. At the same time I noticed with satisfaction that as a Swede one could always expect a more open behaviour than could several other foreigners, who in recent times, through the secret export of models, and by tempting away the workmen, etc, have aroused the most reasonable suspicions against themselves. On account of these and other avaricious tricks the industrious and honest Englishman is on his guard; but one does him an injustice if one believes that he makes secrets of things other than those whose publication would be detrimental to his interests; every wise tradesman in another country would also not willingly allow such things to be made known. The Englishman is, on the contrary, in no way reticent when he encounters someone who knows what he is talking about, and one can be fairly certain that neither out of loquaciousness nor out of deceit will he say more or less than he knows.

Chapter 5

The North-East

IT WAS NATURAL, FROM NOW ON, SINCE I HAD BEEN LEFT TO myself, to direct my attention chiefly to those ironworks which I had not yet had an opportunity of seeing, and which I could encounter on my further journey to Scotland. I knew already before my departure from London that some important ironworks lay in the neighbourhood of Sheffield, in the little town of Rotherham, and in several places in the southern part of Yorkshire, but I had no more been able to get any reliable information than to obtain introductions to the proprietors. It was therefore my intention to go to Hull, in order to get the necessary letters from consul Brandström there, and in the meantime, to see as much in passing as I could. I therefore took a seat in the Mail Coach direct to Sheffield, which constitutes a day's journey or about 12 Swedish miles.

Near to Birmingham, or so long as one is in Warwickshire, and almost until one approaches Derby, the countryside is fairly flat; afterwards come small hillocks, which increase more and more, as when one approaches Chesterfield, and continue all the way to Sheffield. The eminences, which rise in the shape of hills and give to the district a singular appearance, are, like the valleys lying between them, either cultivated or covered by beautiful deciduous woodland. Upon this alteration of the landscape chalk quarries and limekilns also showed in the distance, as well as one or two ironworks and some coalmines. I had not known before that any blast furnaces existed in Derbyshire; I afterwards heard, however, that there are several there, the production of which, however, in respect of size, is not to be compared with that of those previously reported upon.

It was already dark before I got to Sheffield, and I could thus not see anything of the town and the surrounding district. I therefore decided to devote a few hours of the following day to obtaining at least a superficial knowledge thereof. However, I had the opportunity, upon dismounting from the coach, of making the acquaintance of a Quaker, who was a shareholder and manager of an ironworks in the town; he sought me out on the following morning and accompanied me to several ironworks.

Sheffield is one of the smaller towns of England, but very populous and famous on account of its cast steel factories and of the quantity of silverware and cutting tools which are made there. Through the middle of the town runs the river Don, the fall of which is utilised by the rolling-, cutting-, and polishing-works erected here. Round about and even in the town are coalmines, from which the transport to some places is facilitated by railways. The goods made here must, it is true, be transported for some English miles on wheels, because the river is not navigable, and there are also no canals which come up to the neighbourhood of the town; when, however, one considers the value of the goods, and realises that most of the requirements for the factories and buildings are on the spot, it is easy to see that a small amount of land transport is of little importance.

Also in no place in England can one buy such cutlery, of such a quality and at such a price, as here, and one often buys knives, scissors, etc, in London, under the name 'town made work' (that is, work made by natives in the town), which are made in Sheffield and upon which either a well-known cutler of the capital has had his mark impressed, or which have been so stamped by others behind his back. In London this is pretty generally known, and as far as concerns razors, I have found it out by experience. I bought there from several cutlers a few dozen razors for myself and for several friends, for which, without regard for the handles or mountings, I paid up to half a guinea each, but I soon found that there was scarcely a single one amongst them which equalled in quality the razors from Sheffield, of which I could have bought a hundred dozen at $2\frac{1}{2}$ English shillings each at an ironmongers in Wapping. Some English people told me that the same thing had happened to them with penknives and scissors. When one knows how difficult it is, in the large-scale manufacture of such things, to obtain a quantity of exactly the same quality, the foregoing seems to prove much to the advantage of the Sheffield factories.

However, another kind of cutting ware is made here which even though the factories do no substantial trade in it, yet gives rise to it at second and third hand. These goods are *cast* in moulds, ground and polished like other steelwork, and often have a sharp edge, but break at the tiniest pressure. I have seen razors, scissors, table knives and forks of this kind with a fine polish, the nature of which, however, a practised eye can easily discover. Some of these articles can be sold fifty per cent cheaper than the equivalent work in steel, and in recent times a quantity of them has been exported to both Indies and to several places in Europe. However, the true English patriot is not happy about this trade, because it proportionately diminishes the profits of those who make the good products, and because, through misuse of these goods, the confidence in the otherwise justly famous English cutting wares may be weakened. Yet the invention remains of value, partly because it in general demonstrates the nature of the iron, and partly because it can certainly be used for some purposes without harm.

Besides the cutlery factories here, the above-mentioned ironworks, which lies on the river in about the centre of the town, should be noticed. It consists of a trip hammer of the Swedish type, approximately like the one already described at Coalbrookdale, some hearths, furnaces, rolling and cutting mills, etc. Some of these are driven by water, others by steam engines. In the main they are here engaged upon forgings for other works, like certain rough machine parts, material for tools, and things of that kind; iron sheets of all dimensions and qualities are made to order; cast steel is drawn and rolled, etc. I saw here plates of the unusual dimensions, 5 feet long by 2 feet wide, and somewhat thicker than the normal Swedish plates. My guide, Mr Smith, who had recently obtained this order, did not know himself what they were supposed to be used for. In another workshop cast steel was rolled into sheets about 2 feet long, 10 to 12 inches wide, and about 1/16 inch thick, which were afterwards cut diagonally into saw blades. Also I saw cast steel bars a line* in thickness and some inches wide, cut into rods about $\frac{3}{8}$ inch wide with a normal slitting mill, from which afterwards the blades of pen-knives were forged. The sheets were very moderately heated in a normal sheet heating furnace, and as they were taken out, they were struck, with a peculiar skilled movement, on the surface of a cast-iron anvil buried in the floor of the forge. Afterwards they were put under the rolls several times, forwards and backwards; the rolls were 9 inches in diameter, rather more than two feet long, well polished, and were screwed together a little each time a sheet went through. When the sheets came out from under

---

*An old measurement, equal to about 1/12 in—Eng. trans.

cast-steel works, which has long been famous, is that of Mr Huntsman in Sheffield. His brand has won general credit in the whole of Europe, and the products of the other works have only been comparable for a few years.

While they were here zealously working to bring it to the same degree of perfection as Huntsman, they discovered more and more of the nature of this peculiar material, and at last found that everything depended upon the quality of the raw material and upon precision in the melting. Meanwhile, in these experiments, and even now through accidental occurrences, results quite other than those expected were obtained, but the causes are now known, and a practical knowledge of the material itself ensures that wrought iron or steel is no longer sold as cast steel. The trace elements, which have such a fundamental effect on wrought iron and steel at unusually high temperatures are perhaps not yet perfectly known, and the small details which determined the nature of the products resulting in the preparation of cast steel, escaped the English workers for a long time, just as they are still unknown to the chemists who have written about cast steel. Clouet, who presumably had been led to his experiments by Vandermonde's, Berthollet's and Monge's excellent treatises on iron, had, in spite of his skill as a savant and observer, not paid attention to some details which gave him a result conflicting not only with the best and only fitting theory of iron we have, but also with experience in various large-scale iron processes. Mushet, who was supposed to have repeated these experiments, again got other results, but was, just like his predecessor, misled by some unimportant details, which led him to propound his own theory of iron, the application of which on a large scale convinced him, with great loss, of his error.[14] When, however, one goes attentively through these two men's reports on their experiments, one is always brought a step nearer to the truth, and must properties of it. A cutler, Petitvall, who sold expensive and unserviceable razors at the exhibition of manufactures in the Louvre, proved by word and deed that he had not earned the gold medal which he had received the previous year for his supposed skill in working cast steel. It is only necessary to place these razors beside the English ones, or beside those of Scharff and Major Nordwall, in order to find great differences with a moderately practised eye. The French workers merely excel in the working of shear steel, and they carry this to a very advanced state, for if one excepts the polish, which is not so pleasing on this kind of steel, one finds cutting instruments made from it which, for certain purposes, are still superior to those which are generally made of cast steel. In England on the other hand the practical knowledge of the last-mentioned type of steel is much more general. One encounters little cutlery there which is not made from it, and on my whole tour, as well as in my stay in London, I was not able to see a single saw, from the large, several feet long carpenters' saws to the smallest surgical ones, which were not made of a type of cast steel, with broad blades, and quite unlike the ones used in Sweden, Germany, and France. From this it almost seems that for the nations which want to compete with England in steel manufacture, it is more important to get to know the uses of cast steel, and to accustom the workers to it, than to make it themselves, but then the import of it must not be prohibited, or loaded with a heavy duty.

A few English miles from Sheffield, on the way to York, lies the little town of Rotherham in a beautiful district on the River Don, which is navigable through locks up to the Humber and to the sea for so-called lighters of about 70 tons. On these small vessels, which are very similar to the Scheeren [Sweden] boats, although more strongly built, Swedish and Russian iron, boards, beams, tar, as well as several Baltic products, are brought from Hull and along the coast, and either used in Rotherham or landed there for further transport overland to Sheffield and other places. The return loads consist of the products of the iron and steelworks here, of burnt lime and coal, as well as Sheffield manufactured goods. The district around is intensively cultivated, and the fields are crossed in several places by little tracks which connect the coalmines with the ironworks, glassworks, and limekilns in the neighbourhood and in the town. The houses here are built partly of brick, partly of squared stone, and some are roofed with a shaly sandstone, which comes out of the river, and which I never found to be used for this purpose anywhere else.

Besides two blast furnaces and foundries near the town, belonging to a Mr Walker, there is also in the town a large works, which consists of some refineries, puddling, and ball furnaces, as well as the associated rolling mills and a trip hammer of the Swedish type. In the construction and equipment of this latter works there was nothing specially remarkable, but the process, of which more in its place, differed somewhat from that which I had previously seen. The iron smelted here is said to be better than ordinary English iron, and it indeed has that appearance. Among other things made from it were spade blades, almost $3\frac{1}{2}$ inches wide and 5 to 6 inches long. These spade blades consisted of two iron bars placed together and completely welded together with a piece of scrap steel inset in the forge, except at the upper end, where an opening was left for the shaft; they were afterwards rolled out to the required size, cut, cold hammered, and finished by hand. At this works they had tried out a process which was very similar to our Walloon process, and by means of which they had obtained an excellent iron, but on account of the lack of charcoal, which is here so expensive that the production costs could by no means be covered, they had had to give up the work.

This works also has ten steel furnaces, in which about 1,000 tons, or 7,500 shippound of Swedish Oregrund iron and 300 tons of Russian iron of the Old Sabel mark[17] are refined annually. The construction of these furnaces was fairly similar to that of the reverberatory furnaces introduced by the late mining superintendent Rinman in Sweden, with the difference that the former had one or at the most two chambers, and therefore agree more closely with those described by Jars. A double furnace with two chambers takes eight to nine tons. Usually eight days are required for preparing the furnace and loading the iron, eight days for firing, and as long again for cooling down. In one such furnace therefore, if it operates throughout the year, on average about 140 tons or rather more than 1,000 shippounds of steel can be made. The cementation material consists here, as with us, of hardwood charcoal, with a little ash.

I have never been able to imagine, and likewise I know of no real explanation by anybody, what purpose the ash serves here, or how it is supposed to act upon the iron. I have an idea that it merely serves to dilute the charcoal, which would otherwise give out its carbon too quickly, over-enrich the surface of the bars with it, and obstruct the penetration of the same to the core. Yet they also said here, that often no ash was added, if they could get charcoal from branches or young wood. This gives upon burning ashes with the most potash. Might its content of potash, therefore, just like that of the usual ash, have an effect in steel refining which is as yet unknown to us?

I have mentioned previously, that I had no special introductions either here or at Sheffield. It was therefore a mere accident that I saw these works and at the same time was able to make the acquaintance of one of the manufacturers, through whom I obtained important information about the Swedish iron, and with whom I have opened a correspondence which, upon a longer continuance, can be useful and instructive for both sides.

After I had stayed in Sheffield and Rotherham a few days longer than I had at first intended, and had in this time seen the most remarkable things, I travelled with the post direct to York, from where another post coach departs every night at 1 o'clock for Hull. From Rotherham to York it is about eight Swedish miles through the towns of Doncaster, Thorne, Snaith, and Selby, and thence to Hull a further six miles, through Beverley. Although this is not by a long way the shortest route, it is yet that upon which one certainly travels the fastest, which was now my principal object. Had my time allowed of it, or had I been able, upon my departure from London, to obtain addresses in Barnsley, Wakefield, Bradford, and Leeds, I would have taken this way, upon which there are several important ironworks, foundries, and factories of all kinds. Also in the last-mentioned district there are rich coal seams, canals, and many another installation which deserves the attention of a travelling miner and metallurgist, of which, however, nothing is to be encountered on the way which I took, although the district is otherwise beautiful and well cultivated, and the towns clean and populous. I did indeed think to make up for this loss on another occasion, but I began more and more to see that a traveller who cannot spend at least three years in England, must often restrain his curiosity, and let much go by, in order to be able to see and to observe something worth while.

The town of Hull, which may well deserve the third place among the English trading towns, has in the last few years risen to an almost unbelievable degree of prosperity through the extended trade and manufacture of Great Britain. In order to convince oneself of this, one needs only to cast a glance at the town itself, where in the course of a few years several new streets have been laid out and built up with fine houses, the number of which increases daily. Its situation is very suitable in respect to the navigation with small vessels on the Humber, and on account of the many navigable rivers and canals connected with it and which extend farther inland; only the entrance is difficult, the roadsteads exposed to certain winds, and the docks or inner harbour very confined for loading and unloading. A fund has therefore been raised by subscription for dock construction, which has recently been begun, and which ought to be ready for a few hundred ships in three years. For this construction the interested parties have bought the land, and paid up to two guineas per square yard for a part of it. Meanwhile, the Swedish consul Brandström with a company, has founded a dock for about seventy ships on the other side of the Humber, nearer to the sea, at Great Grimsby, where he has already, in not quite two years, loaded and unloaded 25 of his own ships, the cargoes of which have brought in over £10,000 sterling to the Crown.

Hull carries on an intensive import trade with Sweden, Norway, and the Baltic, with tar, boards, beams, iron, hemp, etc, and exports manufactured goods of all kinds to these regions. I saw here various kinds of Swedish bar iron, among which some brands, especially in recent years, have distinguished themselves as less good, partly by the presence of some redshortness, and partly through bad forging. Others, of good material, were badly forged, and heavier than they should have been according to the given dimensions; a circumstance which, although it may seem to be unimportant to several ironmasters, yet has a great influence upon the sales. A ship's smith, who worked for Consul Brandström, tested several bars in my presence, which were so redshort that I believed at first that the mark was counterfeit, which I had already seen in Cornwall, and afterwards heard about in other places. When or where such forgery takes place, is unknown to me, at least no such thing happened at those ironworks to which I was permitted free entry. I would rather believe that this illicit industry, by which more damage is done to the English manufacturers than to the Swedish ironmasters, is carried on where either no Swede at all is admitted, or where he has to gain entry by many roundabout ways. The false marks are easily recognised by their great smoothness, and sometimes by the form of the stamp, which is here oblong or four-cornered, whereas the Swedish ones are round and clumsily engraved, whereby the stamp appears rough, and beside this are often effaced or damaged in the polishing. If a commercial speculation founded upon the deception of the English customs system has given rise to such a fraud on a large scale, and is said still to be doing so, then such a thing can probably not long escape the attention of the English government, since the latter must soon find out its effects on the refining of the iron and on several manufactures, for which reliable and good iron is requisite. Otherwise it is very usual in England to find marks of all kinds imitated; if, however, the buyer often obtains better and almost always just as good wares under these marks as under the genuine ones, he has nothing at all to complain about, and this little industry only affects the other manufacturers. For this reason the Portuguese and Italians cannot say anything about our steel marks, and also those countries whose brands are imitated by us can be regarded as less injured, seeing that their little works are not adequate to satisfy an increased requirement. When, however, really bad iron is exported under Swedish marks which previously had good materials; when poorer kinds of iron are only differentiated from the best with one or two points or by the different placing of the same figures— then this, although it is only a mere modification of counterfeiting, is perhaps more generally disadvantageous to our trade than the deception mentioned above.

engines were here made upon the same principles as those in Sweden in recent years, only with the difference, that in these there is more iron, and all the wheelwork is cast, so that at the same time they occupy less space and can be more easily taken to pieces and transported.

At the shipyard in Hull the above-mentioned cast-steel saws were in general use. The largest, or so-called board saws (whipsaws), for cutting the baulks, were five feet long, $\frac{1}{2}$ to $\frac{3}{4}$ line thick, 5 inches wide at the top and $2\frac{1}{2}$ to 3 inches at the bottom; the more than half-inch long teeth were filed slanting and crosswise, so that one tooth had its cutting edge on the right and the next on the left. With such a handsaw two people could cut 540 feet of 9 to 10 inch thick pine baulk daily, the time for filing the teeth being counted in. Here as at the new docks, work began at 7 o'clock in the morning, and finished at 6 o'clock in the evening. This is the usual working period in England, and is adequate for anyone who wants to use his strength properly. In general I think that I have met the same methods with the English workers, particularly the workers on the land, etc, as with the Dalekarlians, that is, to work not vigorously, but evenly, and not to spend so much time upon preliminary preparations for easing or expediting the work.

Round about the town were various well-built windmills, which were all so equipped that they oriented themselves according to the wind.

In order to get from Hull on to the great post road to Newcastle upon Tyne, one must return to York. The countryside between the latter town and Hull is very flat, and consists mostly of low-lying meadows cut through by broad water ditches, which a tourist might easily take for canals; the purpose of which, however, is merely to drain the land. The town of York has few factories or none at all, and is merely remarkable on account of its many beautiful churches in the gothic style, and on account of its former greatness and its appearance, which is still partly preserved by the nobility and landed gentry living round about, who spend the winter there.

From here to Newcastle it is almost 13 Swedish miles through the towns of Easingwold, Thirsk, Northallerton, Darlington, and Durham. Around the River Tees, which divides Yorkshire from Durham, and still through the latter county, meadows alternate with hills and valleys, which extend farther than those described so far, and thus give the countryside a certain similarity to a part of Kalmar Län or some districts of Värmland, north of Karlstad. On the Tees, as well as on the River Wear, around the town of Bishop Auckland, there are said to be rich coal seams, which have indeed been investigated by borings, but not yet worked. At Chester le Street, approximately half-way between Durham and Newcastle, one already begins to notice coal mines, which afterwards continue along the banks of the Wear down into Sunderland. Near to New-castle one comes to the famous deposits which are worked on both sides of the River Tyne from Shields to Limming-ton [Lemington], over a distance of a Swedish mile. From these and from the above-mentioned rich seams on the River Wear above Sunderland, almost the whole of London is supplied with coal, and further substantial quantities are exported to the north, to France, to the Mediterranean, and the West Indies.

The town of Newcastle, where this far-reaching commerce is mainly concentrated, can also be regarded as the centre point of the important seams, because it is surrounded on all sides by coal mines. Since these seams as well as the work there carried out are already completely and reliably described in Jar's *Metallurgical Tour* [Gabriel Jars, *Voyages Métallurgiques* (3 vols., Lyon & Paris, 1774-81)] and in the English encyclopaedias, I will here merely put in enough about them to enable the reader to gain a general conception.

The best and most considerable seams lie about 90 fathoms deep, almost horizontally, and are rarely more than 5 feet thick. The deposits which are encountered between the coal consist of several variants of shale and sandstone. Sometimes thin deposits of iron ore are met with, in appearance the same as those of Merthyr Tydfil. The iron ore rarely occurs in balls, which are so general in the coal mines in Staffordshire, Shropshire, and Scotland. The seams are often cut through, compressed, or thrown out of position by so-called dykes, or large masses of rock, sometimes of a type of basalt (Mr Werner's greenstone), sometimes of a fine, dense, and white-yellow or grey kind of stone. An example of such a distortion occurs in the Montagu coal mine, where the seam close to the barren rock (dyke) stands almost vertically, or with a 1 foot fall in 3 feet. Above Newcastle these rock masses occur more frequently, until they completely break up the coal. Also the seams themselves are less regular, and the coal in general worse, so that, if the coals from the mines in and below the town are sold for 26 shillings, these often do not command more than 18. (The chaldron here is in proportion to the London one as 15 is to 8.) At Montagu, real coke, or carbonised coal, is encountered next to the barren rock (dyke) at a depth of 37 fathoms, and at the same depth, a few fathoms away, a substance which is quite similar to wood charcoal, which, over a distance of half an English mile, changes first to ordinary coal (pit coals) and afterwards into a firmer kind, called stone coals. At Walker coal mine, below the town, there is found next to one of the intrusive wedges not only coke, but also a substance which looks like volcanic ash. Perhaps this latter material occurs more often than is believed, although it mostly escapes the attention of the workers. At least, I have in several places amongst the coals which are sold in London, found clear traces of the charcoal-like substance described above.

At Walker in the so-called King's pit is a salt spring, the water from which is taken to a nearby soda factory, of which I shall say more below. The inflow of water in the mines around Newcastle is very considerable, and is controlled by steam engines of 50, 60, and up to 100 horse-power.

At Long Benton the whole of the haulage of coals from a 95 fathom deep gallery is performed by a large, double-bucket overshot wheel, which is driven by the mine water pumped to a reservoir above the wheel. The tubs, loaded with a couple of tons of coal, went from the filling point up to the pit bank in less than $1\frac{1}{4}$ minutes. As soon as the full tub came up, it was uncoupled by a man and an empty one attached in its place; the first one was now run a few yards farther on rails, emptied, and brought back to the shaft before a fresh tub came up. They proceed in just the same manner at the mines where the haulage is done by steam engines, and if the coal has to be taken some distance from the mine, they travel at full gallop, so that man and horse are back again to receive the ascending tub. In order to hold back the water which would otherwise penetrate the walls of the shaft, they are all timbered and covered with boards, or also, which is now the most usual, lined with bricks or hewn sandstone, to a diameter of 8 to 9 feet. In some places they are built of cast-iron cylinders, of which one fits into the other, several fathoms deep. The cost of sinking and lining a shaft to the large coal seams, which lie 90 fathoms or so deep, is usually reckoned at £6,000 to £8,000 sterling or more. They therefore make shift to carry out the work below ground as far as they can, until there is no further ventilation, which method of working demands a greater number of horses in the mines. At Long Benton alone there are rails upon which the waggons run, starts a few yards from the shaft. On the other side of the shaft, close to the opening, is a horizontal drum or driving cage, which is so large that an iron rope, half an English mile long, can be wound upon it. At one end of this drum is a large toothed wheel, which engages with a smaller one, on the axle of which a large wooden flywheel is fixed. On the other end is a smaller cog-wheel, which engages with a large one having a common axis with a small drum fixed inside the pit mouth at the edge. Upon this latter a rope 95 fathoms long (which is the depth of the shaft) can be wound, upon one end of which is a large counterweight. When now a loaded waggon is to go down, it is coupled to the iron rope, which is already wound on the large drum, and set into motion upon the plane. As the waggon runs down, and the iron rope is unwound from the large drum, so the one with the counterweight is wound up on the small drum, and the diameters and the unequal speeds of the drums through the gearing, are so adapted that when the waggon has arrived at the predetermined point at the lower end of the plane, the counterweight is at the top of the shaft.

When, in reverse, the empty waggon is to be pulled up again, the counterweight acts, through gravity, upon the small drum, the toothed wheel of which thereupon sets the large one in motion. The counterweight has as much excess weight as is necessary to pull the waggon up, and when the latter has arrived at the upper end of the plane, the bob or counterweight comes to a stop on the floor of the mine. Above the large flywheel is a brake, on the same axis as the large drum, by means of which the speed on the ascent and descent can be moderated, and also the machine is braked when the counterweight is up. They had wanted to fit the Watt governor to this machine, which in any case is well designed, with the intention of moderating the speed without manual strength, but it is not used any more, because one of the people who load the waggons has nothing else to do during the up and down journeys, except to brake. Between the rails of the railway, rollers were fitted every 15 yards, to reduce the wear and tear on the iron rope and the friction. The speed at which the waggons went up and down was the same as that of the English mail coaches, or according to calculation rather more than one Swedish mile an hour.

After the coal has been brought down from the mines to the banks of the Tyne, it is loaded into larger or smaller vessels, according to the position: the large ships cannot go higher up than the Newcastle Bridge. From here, over a distance of a few English miles down to the estuary of the Tyne (Tynemouth) or North and South Shields, loading is mostly done directly into the ships, but the coal from the mines situated above the bridge must first be brought down by smaller vessels.

Besides the mines and the coal trade, through which Newcastle has become so populous and prosperous, there are here, partly in the town itself, partly in the neighbourhood, various other works and industrial undertakings, which deserve mention here, such as ironworks, foundries, mills, potteries, brickworks, spinning mills, white-lead and soda factories, vitriol works, etc. Among these the following are especially noteworthy.

Tyne-Works, an ironworks near Limmington [Lemington], which was formerly merely a foundry, has been substantially extended in recent years. It now consists of two blast furnaces, two large English helve hammers, some puddling furnaces, a rolling mill, and a cupola furnace, as well as several other furnaces and installations which they were engaged in building. The blast furnaces were here of an individual construction, round, and with very thin brickwork. The one furnace which was not in operation, had split, so that the flame shot out a little way below the crown. The blower, which was driven by a steam engine, consisted as usual of a large cylinder with a regulator of the same size, the roof of which was loaded with $4\frac{1}{2}$ pounds on each square inch. This blast was the strongest which I have seen anywhere in England, for 3 or at the most $3\frac{1}{2}$ was otherwise the most usual, and in some places, where they had smaller blast furnaces, and paid more attention to the quality of the iron, the pressure often did not go above $2\frac{1}{2}$ or about 3 pounds. I do not know the actual purpose of this, for although the principal ore was much poorer than in some other places, more of the rich red haematite from Cumberland and Lancashire was added to it, so that the charge did not appear to me to be very difficult to smelt. Presumably this is part of the plan of the method projected here, to make bar iron of a quality equal to the Swedish; but if it is permissible to judge from a tapping which was made in my presence, I would not consider the pig-iron as serviceable for this purpose. In the same way, the bar iron process now in use (the refining method), which differs in certain details from all that I had seen up till now, does not seem to me to be the best-planned one.

Meanwhile, great sums have been expended on these works, upon the experiments as well as the installations. If one is to believe the stories in the town itself, it has already cost the present proprietors, Surtier, Bourdon & Company, more than £150,000. Because this house suspended payment last summer, I do not know whether the buildings, which were planned for a production of at least 1,500 tons, are finished. However, be that as it may, I do not believe that these works will bring about a significant reduction of Swedish sales to England.

The lathe for rolls, which was driven by a steam engine, was here very well arranged. Instead of the turning tool being held by hand, as is usual, it was set in a post of cast iron, which was movable along the length of the lathe and provided with a screw, by means of which the workman could move the tool backwards and forwards at pleasure, always at the same distance.

The vitriol works at Denton between Limmington [Lemington] and Newcastle, belonging to a Mr Thomas, deserve to be seen more on account of the simplicity of their layout and equipment than for anything else. The entire works consist of a boiling house and some cooling vats and reservoirs, all under one roof. Above, in front of the building, is a rectangular flat space of about 100 yards square, upon which hard coal and shale, which contains pyrites, from a nearby pit, are spread out in layers one or more feet thick. The ground in this area slopes down somewhat towards the house, and on this side is a ditch, where all the rain-water, which either falls upon the deposit of coal, or is brought down through it from the hill, is collected. From this ditch the vitriol-containing water is led through channels into a large sump, from which it is tapped into a lead pan, boiled, and brought into the cooling vats, which are at floor level. Small branches and bundles of twigs are hung therein, upon which, as upon the wall and floor of the vat, the vitriol crystallises in quantity. The mother-liquor is finally tapped off and the vats cleaned out for a fresh filling.

Near the vitriol works tar was distilled from coal. The plant was here simpler and not so costly as at Coalbrookdale, and consisted merely of some cylinders of cast iron, which were built horizontally into a furnace of brickwork; the latter was provided with a grate which was fired so that the flames played round the cylinders, which were filled with fresh coal for each burning. The bituminous substances thereby evolved went partly in liquid form, partly as smoke, through a pipe in the lower edge of the cylinder, into a large cask partly filled with water. Another pipe was fixed into the upper end of this cask, and was connected

111

to a smaller cask, which had an opening at the top, through which the hydrogen gas could escape freely. The tar was afterwards poured into a large standing vat, which had several tapping holes one above the other, and there allowed to stand, in order to deposit the impurities and to separate itself from the water. The tar refined in this fashion was finally boiled down to pitch, or used for various purposes just as it was. The tar water was boiled with ochre or colcothar into a paint for fence-posts and the like.[19]

The soda factory near the Walker coalmine, about three English miles below Newcastle, although it is not to be compared in size with several other English factories, yet deserves a foremost place among them on account of its equipment. The soda is here prepared from common salt by decomposition, either with lead or refined potash (the American pearl-ash), and since the chemical principles of this process have already been described with several details in the *Annales de Chemie* and in *Nicholson's Journal*, I will here merely say something about the main layout and the equipment.

We know that in a certain period of the French Revolution several articles of trade rose to an unusually high price, among them Spanish barilla,[20] which was principally used for the preparation of the finest soda. This, taken together with what had been written and tried out in France in connection with the preparation of soda from common salt, gave Lord Dundonald the idea of trying something of the sort on a large scale at Newcastle, where he obtained loans and shareholders, who then, after several unsuccessful experiments, finally brought the process to the state of perfection where a proper works could be set up. A principal circumstance here was, to obtain the salt at a low price, for the tax on salt which is used in England itself is £20 per ton. Therefore the works were founded near to Walker, and an agreement was concluded with the owner of the mine for the use of a salt spring which arises in the mine. Also permission was received from the government to prepare as much salt as was necessary for the factory without any tax. However, none may be sold, under pain of a fine of £500 and loss of the privilege. Hereupon a further agreement was concluded with the mine-owner, that the coal from Walker would be taken at all times for a certain price, in consideration of which the mine-owner was to allow a pump to be fitted to the steam engine for moving the brine, for which, as often as it was in operation, 5 shillings a day was to be paid. By means of this pumping installation the brine is now conducted through channels directly into the pans lying below, about 100 yards from the mine. These pans were, as usual, of Swedish salt-pan sheet, about 10 yards in area and half a yard deep. The manufacturing costs for 1 ton of salt run to 25 to 30 shillings.

The lead necessary for decomposition of the salt must be calcined to a certain degree; more or less calcination causes loss. Lead is therefore bought in metallic form and calcined in the works itself, in furnaces specially built for the purpose. In buying the lead much importance is attached to the silver content, on which account also all the lead used here is tested beforehand. If the lead contains only 8 ounces per ton, or scarcely 1/20 of one per cent, it already repays the cost of refining, because, apart from the yield of silver, one also receives a price higher by 5 shillings for each ton of lead thus refined. The reasons why the silver-free lead commands a higher price, and is especially sought by those who make lead foil, or draw lead into pipes and sheets, consists in its greater softness. One who is properly skilled in the matter can tell the difference merely by cutting a chip from the corner of the bar of lead. Whether this difference can proceed solely from the silver content, or whether the lead, after it has been calcined, has decomposed the salt, and has again been freed from the hydrochloric acid and reduced, has acquired a great malleability in some other way, can, however, not be stated with certainty, for they have not yet tried to use lead without a silver content here.

The soda obtained by decomposition of the salt is caustic, and is carbonated by being placed in a calcining furnace with sawdust, and burnt with constant stirring. The product of this operation is extracted, filtered, and allowed to crystallise in large basins, where the soda deposits on hanging pieces of wood or chips. One often sees here soda crystals 6 to 7 inches long, and as clear as ice. The soda prepared by decomposing the salt with potash occurs in smaller crystals, and perhaps contains something of vegetable potash. Both kinds are sold in bulk at £50 or £60 per ton, and are used throughout England in bleaching muslin, by druggists, and, mixed with soapy water, for washing, to make cotton and linen articles truly white. It is also asserted that a saving is thus made; at least the soda is sold with this claim in several grocery shops in London.

Besides the advantageous situation of this works in respect of the closeness of the salt spring and the coal, several excellent inventions are to be seen in the building itself, to lighten the work and to save wages, such as pumps, channels, railways of cast iron upon which little waggons, likewise of iron, and loaded with lead, coal, or other goods appertaining to the manufacture, are pulled by one workman; further, a mill with vertical stones for pulverising the salt, etc.

The manager of this factory informed me of an observation which deserves to be mentioned here. In building in a salt pan he had, owing to a shortage of Swedish plates, been obliged to have some English ones inserted in the bottom. The smith, who presumably knew from experience the advantages of the Swedish plates, did not want to put in any English ones, but it was necessary, since no others were to be had. When the pan had been in use for a few months, it began to leak, and upon closer investigation it was found that the English plates were partly as though eaten by worms on the upper surface, partly penetrated by small holes, as big as a pin, in some places. After these had been repaired the boiling was continued for some time, but at last the salt mass ate its way right through, and they were obliged to insert new plates. The Swedish plates were on the other hand not attacked at all, although they were no thicker than the others, and to all appearances were far worse, whereas the English ones were rolled throughout and smoother on the surface. Probably the greater or lesser proportion of redshortness which is always inherent in the English iron, and which definitely makes it softer and more inclined to rust, was the cause of this occurrence.

In the town itself, on the River Tyne, lies a small ironworks, belonging to a Mr Winch, where small anchors, bolts, and other kinds of ships' ironwork are repaired and made. Near to this is a grinding mill with three motions, and a powder mill, which was driven by a steam engine. Although one can certainly obtain fairly good millstones here, they are yet imported from France, from the so-called Pierre de Meulon near Paris. A pair of these stones cost up to 60 guineas during the war. The normal price is otherwise 30 guineas for stones of ordinary size; however, this high cost is mostly to be traced to the high duty. These stones are considered to be better than the Rhineland ones, and I am surprised that they have not been introduced instead of the latter in Sweden, since it should be possible to obtain them at low prices via Havre and Rouen. The same steam engine, by which the mill is driven, drives also a small tail hammer, beneath which $\frac{3}{4}$ inch square Swedish iron is rounded into ships' bolts. The construction of this hammer was fairly similar to that of the Swedish bar ham-

115

mers, but it had a round depression in the hammer head as well as in the anvil. A bar of English-rolled $\frac{3}{4}$ inch iron, which was standing next to the Swedish, prompted me to ask whether such was also rounded into bolts, whereupon Mr Winch said that this was indeed the case, and that this bolt-iron was sold for £3 per ton more than English rolled bolt-iron from the same melting. The reason for this increase in price is said to be the improvement which the iron actually obtains through the hammering, and when one knows the peculiar alterations which this metal undergoes as a consequence of the smallest operations, one may not call this assertion in question, although there could also be other reasons.

On the other side of the river lies a white-lead factory, into which, however, no strangers are allowed. It belongs to a baronet, whose name has slipped my memory, but who must draw a substantial profit from it, because the white lead produced here has been found to be better than any made anywhere else in Europe. During my stay in France it was praised to me as unusually good, and one could not even guess which method is used here, or whether the advantages of this white lead stem merely from the raw materials.

In a town where people are so occupied with extensive trading, mining, and manufacture, there seems to be almost no time left for the sciences. Yet there are here several experts and amateurs of minerals, among whom Mr Winch, Colonel Bigge (a local Justice of the Peace), George Losch, and Thomas, who all possess nice collections, should be mentioned. An institution almost upon the same plan, although less extensive, as the Royal Institution in London, has admittedly not yet quite come to completion, but promises much for the future. It had, however, progressed so far that chemical and physical lectures were held on certain days of the week; also a fine library had already been created, a collection of minerals purchased, which was increased daily, and several expensive instruments ordered. Mr Thomas Bigge had shown the usefulness of and the need for such an establishment in a pamphlet published in 1802 [Thomas Bigge, *On the Expediency of Establishing, in Newcastle upon Tyne, a lectureship on subjects of Natural and Experimental Philosophy* (Newcastle, 1802)], and within a few months so much had been collected by subscription, that the lectures could be started, which are now given by a very skilled man, the minister of the local Unitarian church, Mr Wil. Turner. Here, just as in London, I found the lectures to be attended by people of all ranks, of every age, and by a large number of ladies, which latter likewise exhibited close attention, notwithstanding that some of them had quite innocently expected something different.

Besides this institute there was also another for the reading of journals and newspapers, which was supported in just the same manner by subscriptions from the townspeople and the gentry living in the country around. The house belonging to this was one of the finest in Newcastle, and so spacious, that some hundreds of people could congregate there.

During my short stay here I enjoyed several samples of English hospitality, especially with Mr Thomas Bigge, on whose estate, Little Benton, I spent several pleasant days.

In order to see the remarkable iron bridge over the River Wear, an excursion was made to the town of Sunderland, a few English miles from Newcastle. This is the largest and finest iron bridge which has yet been built anywhere. It is 236 English feet long between the two ends of the arch, and so high that three-masted vessels can sail away under it with full sail. Everywhere in England one comes across engraved drawings, views, and descriptions of this bridge, and at the inn where I stopped at midday, the bills were embellished with an engraved view of it.[21]

The usual way from Newcastle to Edinburgh amounts to rather more than 17 Swedish miles, through the towns of Morpeth, Alnwick, Belford, and Berwick in Northumberland, and further through Dunbar in Scotland. The landscape is here in general uneven, and consists of long valleys, which are enclosed by hills more extensive and less steep than one usually encounters in England. The fields are large and more open, and divided into large estates or farms, so that the country on the whole has much similarity to certain districts of Sweden, except that there are here few or no woods. This is especially true of parts of Northumberland between Newcastle and Berwick. As soon as one is in Scotland, bare and steep crags arise, partly on the coast out of the sea, partly out of the fields themselves, and rather like the mountains in the Scheeren of Bohuslän, although these are more often of a kind of granite, whereas the former are always of shale, basalt, and like rocks of the second order. The nearer one gets to Scotland, the rarer become the brick houses and around Berwick few houses are to be seen other than those of sandstone, or smaller buildings of a shaly black type of stone, laid in just the same manner as the greystone walls in Sweden.

On my departure from Newcastle I did not want to travel with the mail coach any farther than to Berwick, between which town and Dunbar there occur various basalt outcrops which deserve attention; but when I arrived there, all the rooms were occupied on account of the forthcoming Assizes, and I therefore had to continue my journey through the night. Here I had the misfortune, for the first and last time on my journey through England, to travel with a drunken driver, who, under the pretence of letting his horses recover their breath, increased his state of intoxication several times between each station. The post escort (mail guard), who in this matter seemed to be a true comrade, was finally called into the coach to keep company, where he manoeuvred so clumsily with his loaded gun and pistols that we were all certainly in greater danger than anyone who had wanted to take this opportunity of robbing the mail. A passenger in such a situation would, by reference to the postal regulations, have been able to call for order; however, after I had, in a convenient manner attained possession of the gun, and besides that was not deliberately insulted, I considered it safer to let a small disorder pass, than by my remonstrances perhaps to give rise to a greater one.

Chapter 6

Scotland

DUNBAR IS A SMALL, UNIMPORTANT TOWN CLOSE TO THE SEA. The district around is hilly, and at the entrance to the harbour dangerous rocks rise up, several of which consist of fairly regular basalt pillars. The basalt is reddish, not only on the surface, but often deep in the core of the pillar, but at the same time I did not find any that were red throughout, such as Jameson has claimed to have found.

Outside the town was a quarry in a shaly reddish sandstone, which was used for houses, paving stones, etc. This stone was split out by wedges in large blocks, and afterwards dressed with chisel and maul.

On the coast a seaweed is collected, which is dried and burnt to so-called kelp, which serves instead of barilla in the English soap factories, glassworks, and several other manufactories. It does not by far contain so much soda as the barilla, but it is cheaper, and can therefore often be used with advantage. Kelp is burnt on the entire Scottish coast, particularly, however, on the islands, concerning which further information can be found in an article, 'A tour to the Northern Islands, and particularly to the Island of Sky', by Mr Jameson.[22]

On the road between Dunbar and Edinburgh one sees several fine estates, and in some places the land has an unusually fertile appearance, in so far as I was able to notice this on a fast journey through and in the falling darkness.

Edinburgh occupies a distinguished position among the towns of Great Britain not merely as the old capital of Scotland, but it may be able to vie with most European towns on account of its unique and beautiful situation, its pleasing buildings, and its extensive trade. It is divided into the old and the new towns, which are separated from each other by a deep valley, over which two high bridges have been built. The old town is throughout narrow and unclean, with crooked streets, and built upon steep slopes, so that some houses, which have only four or five storeys on one alley, can present to another a façade of twelve to thirteen. A few large streets are exceptions to this. They are broader and beyond all comparison cleaner than most streets in Paris, and have some magnificent buildings, among which the University building, which is not yet complete, will certainly surpass most of the public buildings in England in taste and elegance.

The new town was founded in recent times [1767] according to a regular plan, with broad and straight streets and a large market place. Few houses of brick are to be found here, but most of them are built of dressed stone, and generally in a higher and nobler style than in the English towns. Also this part is occupied by the well-to-do inhabitants of Edinburgh, or by gentry from the neighbouring countryside, who spend a part of the year here. The extension of this town in a short space of time, and the many buildings which were now complete, bear adequate witness to its extensive trade and its industry, which shows itself even more clearly at Leith, about a Swedish quarter-mile away, on the sea. Leith actually forms the port of Edinburgh, and was formerly regarded as a separate place, but is now connected to the old town of Edinburgh by the many buildings along Leith Walk, so that the two can be considered as a single built-up town, about three-quarters of a mile long and a quarter of a mile wide.

Something which has greatly contributed to the building of the town is the plentiful supply of excellent sandstone, which can be easily procured from the nearby quarries. There is just as little lack of limestone, and in excavating the foundations in the new town they have in many places merely to clear away a few inches of top soil, below which are encountered deposits of sandstone, chalk, and other types of rock, which serves as a sure foundation, and with which one can build above ground. The method of preparing the mortar was new to me. Freshly burnt lime was broken, with a club or staff, into pieces of the size of a walnut, mixed with sand in the appropriate proportions, then water was poured on and the mass stirred with a spade during the slaking process. This work was performed in a level place in the open air, and no more is slaked at one time than a workman can comfortably deal with. After the passage of an hour, and after the mortar had developed the proper heat, it was shovelled on to a large heap, which was kept ready permanently at the building site, where it was allowed to remain lying for some weeks, in order, as the workmen said, to ripen. This heap was often in the open, and was merely covered lightly with boards in rain or strong sunshine. When the mortar was to be used, the part of the heap which had lain long enough was taken and worked into small portions, and the mortar was now tough and tractable, and could be worked better than any mortar which I have seen in Sweden. It was said that a five or six weeks stay in the heaps gave the best mortar, and that they preferred not to use it until it had lain for 14 days, which, however, had to depend greatly upon the weather and the season. Now whether the firmness of the plastering and the masonry which were noticed here, stem from this method of preparation or from the nature of the lime, I cannot say with certainty; only this much is certain, that it far surpasses anything of ours.

I later found that this method of preparing mortar was very usual in England, with the exception of a few small variations. In this connection I must also mention that the English and Scottish bricklayers at any time use a stiffer mortar, spread it thinly and evenly upon the stones, and in general employ more thought than most of our so-called master builders and their workmen, who, under cover of master's certificates and trade unions, bungle one building after another.

The University of Edinburgh is too well known to need any description by me here. It is known that few universities in Europe have had more famous teachers in a shorter time, and that in few high schools have so many skilled men been educated for the State and for the sciences in recent times. Foreigners who completed their studies here have never had cause to regret the time and expense. In order not to depart from my purposes, I shall merely say something about the present state of chemistry and mineralogy.

Chemical lectures are given by the present professor of chemistry, Dr Hope. I attended one of them, which was delivered with the tidiness which is usually observed in England, and with such clarity that I, although I was less used to the language, yet did not lose a single word. Dr Hope combines with this fortunate gift an extensive knowledge of practical chemistry, medicine, mineralogy, and geology. His explanation of Hutton's System of the formation of our earth contained a large number of facts which shed much light upon this subject, although they did not in principle always prove what they were supposed to prove, to confirm this system according to the wishes of its originator. Perhaps innumerable observations are still necessary before we can hope to get a geological system which is general for all rocks and strata on the whole globe; at least, we have so far no single one which does not contradict everyday experience if one wants to apply it to its logical conclusion, no matter how true and illuminating it may be as long as only a small patch of the earth's surface is being considered. Dr Hope also possesses a nice collection of minerals, particularly of those graduated steps which serve to illustrate the above-mentioned subject.

The mineral collection of the University could not now be seen, as it was being moved into the new building mentioned above. Besides that it was under the supervision of a professor, who had the misfortune to lose his sight several years ago, and no one had yet been nominated in his place. It is said, however, that Mr Jameson (about whom something was said above) [p120] has been suggested for this position, and one would have difficulty in finding a more capable man for it. In him one finds combined all the knowledge which is required to bring the science of mineralogy into a more certain and definite form than has been the case hitherto. He is a chemist, mineralogist and geologist, not merely through reading, but through hard-won experience in these disciplines, which one often misses in the authors of mineralogical and geological systems. He is fully acquainted with Herr Werner's system, and he has himself studied in Freyberg under this great master, to whom at least one cannot deny the honour that he has trained a great number of able pupils, and has given to mineralogy a form which is of great use in its application, as well as that through him a geological system has been set up which departs from Nature less than any other, and certainly indicates the way to perfection.

Dr Murray, teacher of chemistry, gives occasional lectures on mineralogy; he is an active and knowledgeable man, and has a nice little collection of minerals.

Besides the collections mentioned above, there are various ones which belong to amateurs. A young banker, Mr Th. Allan, has recently started one, which is already rather good, and increases daily. It is arranged according to the system of Haun, whose lectures he has frequented.

The mountains in and around Edinburgh are remarkable no less on account of their appearance than on account of the rock types which they contain, which all belong to the second order, and consist mostly of basalt, hornblende, shales, etc, in uneven modifications. Among the rare minerals there are prehnite, leucite, and several others. At Arthur's Seat, a mountain which rises with steep slopes to a fair height at one end of the town, there are some reddish crystals, as large as peas or small nuts. These resemble feldspar in some respects, but in other ways are nearer to leucite. These are described by Lametherie in his *Journal* [J. C. de La Métherie, *Journal de Physique*], and were regarded by him as a special species, which he called 'leucite-feldspathique'.

On some excursions with Messrs Jameson and Allan I got to know the mountains round about reasonably well; however, because a circumstantial description of the same would take up too much space here, I omit it, all the more willingly since it would in any case only appear as incomplete and uncertain if it were to be compared with that which we are soon to expect from Mr Jameson.[23]

The mountains otherwise contain neither coal, metals, nor other materials which were immediately connected with the purpose of my tour, with the exceptions of chalk and sandstone, of which I have already made mention. Below the town on the sea coast, and presumably on both sides of the same, there are, however, found the flattened balls of ironstone which are everywhere in the coasts of the Firth of Forth and in Fifeshire collected by poor people and sold to the ironworks at Carron, from which small vehicles are constantly sent out for the purpose.

Neither in the new nor in the old towns are there, so far as I know, any important factories, except a large distillery,

K

and a place where the 'biscuit' for genuine porcelain is painted and gilded.

Since the spirit distillery, as one of the largest and most developed chemical operations, must certainly attract the attention of an investigator of factories; since it takes such a distinguished place in our Swedish economy, and since, finally, the distilleries are among the few Scottish manufacturing establishments which can give an approximate idea of large-scale production, it may be not out of place here to introduce something about the Edinburgh distillery. The spirit prepared here has a somewhat stronger content than the Swedish corn spirit, but is otherwise almost of the same nature. Whether the repulsive taste and smell which the whisky usually has is due to the fact that merely corn, and perhaps not always the best, is taken here, or whether it comes from the method, I cannot make out. I should imagine, however, that it is mainly due to the distillation, which is here done according to a plan which is worked out to save time, and whereby all other advantages are neglected. The primary cause of this is that in Scotland, as with us, the content of the still is taxed, and because the first contracts with the Crown, which were concluded up to a few years ago, did not specify anything with regard to the form of the distilling apparatus, the owners of the distilleries have on their side tried to obtain the greatest advantage therefrom. If these distilleries had had any other advantages, they would certainly have been adopted in England, where the distilleries are now equipped almost the same as ours, the still tax there being paid according to the production, and not according to the size of the still. Anyone who wants more exact information about the equipment of the Scottish distilleries should refer to the *Repository of Arts and Manufactures* [*Repository of Arts, Literature, Commerce, Manufactures, Fashions and Politics*] (Vol. 3, p. 69; Vol. 4, p. 151) where it is illustrated, and to Nicholson's *Journal* or Tilloch's *Philosophical Magazine*, where the main features of the method have been described.[24] However, the following may serve to give a short idea of the above-mentioned distillery.

The stills, which contain only 50 gallons, or nearly 60 Swedish quarts are of copper, a few feet in diameter, but only $1\frac{1}{2}$ to $2\frac{1}{2}$ inches high with head and all. A pipe, a few inches in diameter, rises straight up out of the centre of the still, and afterwards bends, and is connected to the worm in the cooling cask. In this pipe is an upright iron rod, which rests on the bottom of the still, and is equipped with several paddles a little above the bottom. Above, in the pipe, a mechanism is fitted, through which the rod is rotated by two persons, who continuously turn a horizontal handle connected with it. The vanes attached to the end of the rod thus run round in the still, promote evaporation and prevent burning. At the stokehole two other persons stand always ready with shovels and water buckets, and above by the pipe someone constantly takes care that the still does not overheat, and is filled and emptied at the correct time; this is done in every distillery merely by turning two cocks, one of which lets in the mash from a reservoir situated above and the other lets out the spent liquor into a large basin. Upon a given signal of overheating two or three buckets of water are thrown into the firehole, and after one or two minutes, when the overheating has ceased, fresh coal is thrown in to stimulate the fire. If it is desired to push the work to the highest rate, a run can be made in less than six minutes, but usually the filling, distilling, and emptying of the still takes seven minutes and a few seconds, so that a hundred or more distillations can be made in each still in twelve hours.

By the cooling cask, where the spirit runs out, sits a fellow with a glass in his hand, which is filled two or three times in a minute, so that it can be judged from the colour

or other indications when the spent liquor must be tapped
off and fresh mash run in. Thus six persons are needed
to attend a spirit still, and the work seemed to me so ardu-
ous that unusually strong men must certainly be selected
for it, if it is to be carried on day and night with double
teams. I have, it is true, used the word 'mash' above, but
this is not to be understood as being of the same kind as
with us, for the distillation here is merely from wort, from
which the grains are separated just as in the breweries. I
have mentioned in the foregoing, that only corn is used for
distilling. This is immediately malted, and bruised by
means of fluted rollers, which are driven by a steam engine.
The water is afterwards separated in the mash tun on a
movable floor of planks or thin cast-iron plates, which is a
few inches smaller than the fixed floor. Boiling water is
run on to this, and when the wort is good, it is pumped
up by the steam engine, into the cooling vats which take
up the greater part of the upper storey, only one foot deep,
and shaped almost like our corn stooks. From there the
wort is led into the fermentation vats, and finally into the
stills.

The water is heated in two boilers, one of which
holds 10,000 gallons and the other 14,000 gallons, or nearly
18,700 Swedish quarts. The boilers are so installed that
only the cold water has to be pumped up, but after boiling can be allowed to run directly into the mash tun. This
latter was sunk into the floor, of oval form, 23 and 27
feet axes and 5 feet deep. It took a mashing of 16,000 gallons, or nearly 21,300 quarts. This and the fermentation
vats were constructed of upright planks and encircled with
strong iron bands. The latter contained 9,000 to 30,000
gallons. When everything was in full operation, 1,600
gallons of spirit were made daily, and the duty to the
crown had in certain years risen to 80 or 90,000 pounds
sterling. Besides this distillery, there are several more in

Scotland, of which one pays £60,000 and another about £40,000 in duty annually.

At Leith and in several other small places near Edinburgh are various glassworks, foundries, salt boilers, soap and soda factories, paper mills, as well as several similar manufacturing installations, which deserve the attention of a tourist.

The glassworks just outside Leith are especially remarkable, for here is made the clearest and purest crystal glass that one can imagine, and which surpasses in beauty all other, in England as well as in France. There are several, and all very large, but they seem, even with good recommendations, only unwillingly to allow entry to most of the workshops. I only got to see the cutting shop, which consisted of many stones and lathes, which were all driven by one steam engine. The storeroom, where all kinds of cut glass stood exhibited on long tables, was richer and more elegant than any of those of the glassworks which I saw in Paris, although one must give the French their due: their chandeliers, if often of worse materials, are for the most part put together with more taste, and have a more pleasing appearance, than the English ones.

In one of the small streets of Leith there is a soap factory, which belongs to a Mr Jameson, brother of the mineralogist. A foreigner would go past this factory several times without having the least idea of its existence, so little does its outer appearance differ from the usual houses. This is nothing unusual in England, and a stranger is often amazed when within the portal of a small inconspicuous house he finds a bigger warehouse than in the most magnificent factory buildings put up at public expense in other countries. This is also the reason why so few tourists know anything about the English factories, and why often those who have taken the trouble to seek them out have met with failure, if they have not had good addresses. The above-mentioned soap-boiling works was established in the courtyard of two large buildings, and consisted of two lime-kilns, four large boilers or pans, in which the soap was boiled, as well as 96 iron and 20 wooden vessels for preparing the lye.

The limekilns were built on a good plan, to save coal and to effect a uniform burning. They were between 15 and 18 feet high, provided below with three openings to promote the draught and to get the lime out; above was a vault, on one side of which coal and limestone were put through an opening. For the rest, it had the internal configuration, like the English and Scottish limekilns generally, of an upward and downward turned cone, the diameter of which, at the upper end, was almost twice that of the lower base.

The soap kettles were built into furnaces, like brewing pans, and assembled in three distinct sections, of which the lowest, which took up approximately two-fifths of the height of the whole boiler, was a normal, large iron boiler. Upon this a cylindrical centre section of cast iron was fitted with a rabbet, and above that the third piece of timber cask-work, bound with strong iron hoops. All this together thus made up one single boiler, in which 6 to 7 tons or 36 to 40 shippounds of soap could be boiled at one time. Such a built-in boiler cost about £100 sterling.

The iron vessels in which the lye was made, after it had previously been made caustic with quicklime, had the appearance of ordinary cooking pots, but of 6 to 7 feet diameter, and $3\frac{1}{2}$ to 4 feet depth, with walls about 1 inch thick. Each of them weighed $2\frac{1}{2}$ tons or about 18 ship-pounds, and cost £16 sterling per ton. They were cast partly at Carron, partly in a foundry at Leith.

The wooden vessels were larger, but served only for the extraction of the kelp and barilla, for which the iron vessels were likewise used with several advantages.

Besides these vessels, a large basin was sunk into the ground, in which the lye was made caustic with lime; the latter was thereby simultaneously slaked and the mass thus almost brought to the boiling point.

Kelp and barilla were the materials used here for preparing the lye, which, after it had been made caustic, was mixed, under a gentle heating, with Russian tallow and a certain amount of rosin or palm oil, the latter on account of the colour and smell. Potash lye was now no longer' used, because with it only green or soft soap is obtained, which in England has fallen out of use to such an extent that people will hardly use it to wash floors and stairways. The rosin is obtained either by distillation from the resin of the American red pine or from pitch, and in both cases so much turpentine is obtained that this already repays the costs, and the rosin can be sold at the same price as the raw material. The rosin as well as the turpentine from pitch is inferior to that from wood resin. The palm oil, which in most countries is only to be found in the apothecaries, here lay in large barrels, and had cost £6 to £7 sterling per ton. When the soap is boiled, which takes more or less time, according to the purity and strength of the lye, it is allowed to cool, and when it has set to a thick pulp, it is poured into wooden moulds, in which it sets completely hard in 24 or 48 hours. These moulds, of which several are set out in a large room, are 3 feet high, 2 feet long, $1\frac{1}{4}$ feet wide, and put together from 3 inch deep rabbetted frames. When the soap has become hard, the uppermost frame is taken off, and the three-inch thick slice is cut off with a steel wire. Then the second frame is removed, and so the process is carried on down to the floor. The slices are afterwards cut into pieces of 3 inches square section and 12 to 15 inches long with a simple instrument, and packed into wooden casks for sale.

The soap made here is of three kinds: white, yellow,

and brown; however, the colour is merely a variation given to the soap in order to suit the prejudices of the buyers. Venetian soap is also sometimes made, but has now mostly fallen out of use.

The annual production here was about 300 tons, or 1,800 Swedish shippounds, and the price is held between £60 and £70 sterling per ton, including excise duty, which alone runs to £21 per ton, but is not charged on exports. There was a special room in the factory for an excise officer or overseer, who was present all the time, and who evaluated the production from the figures on the forms completed at every boiling. This to all appearances unimportant factory therefore delivers goods to the value of about £19,500 sterling annually.

A few English miles from Edinburgh, near the little town of Dalkeith, there are various coalmines, from which Edinburgh and Leith are partly provided with fuel. The seams are said to extend for several miles in length and width; however, they are often interrupted or compressed by the previously mentioned rock masses (dykes). The coal seams lie completely horizontally, and when they fall, this mostly occurs towards a certain centre point of a large depression, wherein they appear to be inclined on the older mountains, as has also been remarked previously. Among several seams lying one above the other, two in particular are now worked, one of which extends 49 and the other 54 fathoms below ground. The first was 4½ feet thick, and contained worse coal than the latter, which was 5 feet thick. The most important working, which I once inspected in the company of Mr Allan, consists of four shafts, which are sunk within an area of a few hundred square yards. From each of these shafts approximately 150 tons of coal, half large and half small, are brought out weekly. Sometimes the production from one shaft was greater than from the others, and sometimes one of them was shut down, while the work in the other three went on more intensively, so that in general they could reckon for all four shafts upon 300 tons of small coal, and as much large, weekly. Most of the coal was sold on the spot, and taken to Edinburgh by carters, who used ordinary carts for this transport. One such cartload of 4 hundredweights or 448 English pounds, is sold on the spot for 18 pence. The mine water is lifted by steam engines, but the haulage is done by horse whims, which were not particularly remarkable.

At Lasswade, on the way to Dalkeith, I encountered a paper mill, which was not laid out for any great production, but everything, as well as the garden and house in which the proprietor himself lived, was indescribably neat, and well fitted to the locality. The rollers which crushed the rags, and the washing machine, were driven by a steam engine, and the water was led into the works through iron pipes from a brook. The method was, so far as I could observe it in the haste, somewhat different from that at the Swedish paper mills. The rags were sorted, and cut on knives set upright for the purpose in tables fixed to the walls all round the room, which work was done by old people and children. After this the rags were taken to the washing machine, from which the coarser ones went immediately through all the rollers to the vat-house, but the finer ones, after they had passed the heaviest pair of rollers, were put into the bleaching trough. This was in a special house, on either side of a furnace in which six crucibles or earthenware pots, two and two together, could be comfortably set in and taken out. These pots, which were provided with heads from which porcelain pipes went into the trough, were filled with sulphuric acid, common salt, and manganese dioxide in such proportions as to obtain a completely saturated hydrochloric acid [actually, chlorine], which was evolved upon distillation, combined with the water in the paper pulp, and gave the latter the desired whiteness in a short time. The prepared stuff was taken up as usual on moulds, on which a fine mesh of brass wire was stretched. Then it was laid between woollen cloths, where it was pressed, afterwards hung up to dry, scraped, treated with size, dried, and once more pressed. The scraping was done with special knives, sheet by sheet, in order to remove the small lumps and dust solidified in drying. This work was done mostly by young girls, who exhibited a skill therein, by which the English factory workers distinguish themselves from all others. The finished paper of all kinds had a fine appearance, and far surpasses the French and Swedish; it has, however, the same fault as even the best paper nowadays, in that it is more fragile and does not last as long as the old Dutch paper. Presumably this stems from nothing other than the now general use of rollers with knives, which cut through the threads of the rags, instead of the mills and stamps which were formerly used to break them up more along the length and breadth, whereby the paper on drying became more cohesive and got a firmer web.

This is one of the many cases which prove that one often loses in the quality of the goods what one gains in manufacturing price by speeding up the work. In such cases the manufacturer must weigh the pros and cons carefully, for if in the long run he can better dispose of a less good product at a lower price, I do not see why he should spend money upon its improvement, especially since the public is often more concerned with a good buy than a good product. This is quite a different matter from making and selling poor goods under a mark standing in good repute.

On another side of Edinburgh, and also a few English miles away, lies the Cramond ironworks, belonging to Mr Cadell and Sons. It consists of several small workshops, built on a fairly large stream, which is navigable up to the lowest hammer, but which has several little falls higher up, by which rolling mills, hammers, and bellows are operated. Bar iron is not made here in the usual manner, but only old scrap or stock iron is used, which is forged and made up to order as sheets, spades, shovels, and the like. This forged work, and a few hundred shippounds of steel, which are made from Swedish and Russian iron in two furnaces, seems to be the best production of the works. The works consists of two or three forges, one of which contains a helve hammer, the framing, wheels, and other equipment of which were constructed just like the Swedish ones, but with the differences that there were six lifting arms on the cam, and that there was scarcely a single piece of timber in the whole hammer frame. Even the hammer helve was of cast iron, cast in one piece with the head, and had about the thickness of a normal helve. The water wheels, which operated in the undershot manner, some with straight floats, some boarded, were only a few feet high, but were very wide, and assembled from cast iron with rods of wrought iron.

In the hammer-house mentioned, there was a hearth fairly similar to ours, only somewhat larger and with a vault above the fire, by means of which much coal was said to be saved, but which also needed continual repair, notwithstanding that the vault was made of a very refractory stone. To this hearth there belonged a pair of fairly large leather bellows, which were operated by water wheels. A large part of the scrap iron forged into bar iron here is bought in from Holland, and consisted of old nails, horseshoes, and a hundred and one other such things, which are there, as in France and England, partly picked up by poor people from the streets and rubbish-dumps, and partly collected from old ships and timber buildings. Old iron of this kind, as well as the sheet trimmings and the scrap from the spade forge, are put together in so-called piles or cubic heaps, of 11 to 12 inches side, which are heated either in a bloom furnace or in the hearth described above, and afterwards welded together under the large hammer. The assembly of these piles is done merely by children and old people, who have such skill in entangling the pieces of iron one into another that the piles can often be shifted and roughly treated without a nail coming out of them.

The rolling mill, which compared with those in several other places was only small and unimportant, had a heating furnace and a large shear of cast iron, with which the material for the plates and spades was cut up. In the bar forge, where steel, spades, and the like were drawn down, the hammer was of the same construction as the one mentioned previously, but weighed only 15 to 16 Swedish Lis pounds, and had eight lifting arms. The forging of the spades, which here constituted an important article, was done approximately in the following manner. After the spade plates had been cut to suitable length and width, they were drawn down under the smaller hammer to about 7 inches long, 4 inches wide and $\frac{1}{8}$ inch thick. After that they went into a small forge where they were put together two and two, with a piece of scrap steel in the forward end; sand or loam was sprinkled on the other end to prevent welding in the place where the handle fitted in. From here they came back to the hammer, where they were further welded and drawn down to 13 inches long, 7 inches wide, and barely a line thick. After this operation they were brought for the second time into the small forge, where they were finally cut, roughly filed, cold hammered, and provided with handles of ironwood. A dozen of them was sold on the spot for £2 sterling. These spades, which are in general use in England and Scotland, have almost the form of our sand shovels, but are not so long, and rather narrower towards the cutting edge, which is quite straight. I do not doubt that we could make spades of the same kind, and at a better price, if there were no lack of sales.

the coast from Kinghorn up to St Andrews. At one small place, called Elie, red-brown granite is supposed to have been found, but neither my travelling companions nor myself could discover anything of the kind here, and if such really has been found, I would rather believe that it has been brought in with the ballast stones, with which a kind of wall or barrier against the surf has been thrown together.

At Cambo, an estate belonging to Lord Kellie, which lies close to the shore, there was a fair amount of the above-mentioned ironstones, which are collected at the time of the ebb tide, laid in heaps, and taken away to Carron. The sea seems here every year to wash away some of the softer shale in which the ironstone balls lie, and these, when they are laid bare in this manner, are thus thrown on to the beach from time to time, so that in these places several collections can be made in a few years. Near the ironstone seams there were also traces of coal, partly in thin layers, partly forming as it were a crust around the fossilised roots of a sea-growth. These roots, which were now turned into a grey-white fine-grained sandstone, bore on the surface clear indications of their basic form; for the rest they were more or less compressed, and surrounded with a shell of coal, the thickness of which seemed to be more or less proportionate to the degree of petrification. They are always found lying, and often thrown together in heaps without any order, whereas on the other hand another kind of roots from one or two inches in diameter, which resemble bamboo or sugar-canes, invariably stood upright in the shale, were completely round and not surrounded by coal. In the sandstone deposits there occurred also fine veins or, as it were, leaves and stalks of a substance which was exactly like charcoal, just the same as that which, as I have previously mentioned, is so common in the English hard coals.

On the way to Cambo we passed a few small towns and harbours, such as Kirkcaldy, Dysart, Sconie, Largo, Elie, and Anstruther, where the spinning and weaving of coarse canvas seemed, next to fishing, to be the principal occupation of the inhabitants. The houses are here built of stone, and the towns are not so pretty and tidy as they generally are in England, but they must, to judge from the crowds of children with which the streets were teeming, be fairly populous. The country over this whole stretch is highly cultivated, and the fields are laid out in just the same way, and are in several respects worked the same, as with us. It is said that in a short time large meadows have here been brought under cultivation, which is also the case in several other places in England and Scotland; this seems partly to be a consequence of the increased price of grain in the last famine, partly to arise from the present mode of farming, for which the Duke of Bedford has perhaps set the fashion, and which afterwards became so prevalent among persons of rank and substance, not excepting the King himself, who gives a fine example herein on his estates at Windsor. At Cambo seaweed was collected, and used as cattle fodder with great advantage. A single storm could often cast up several hundred cartloads of this fodder on the shore, which is also to be found in Sweden on the coasts of Skåne and Hallands. In a quicksand likewise driven up by the sea, a kind of grass grew, the roots of which made the shore so firm, that people had little concern about this sand.

From Cambo to St Andrews the country maintains the same appearance as before, and the hills, which are there fairly steep on the sea coast, bore several deposits of the types of stone mentioned above. In the town is a school, or a so-called college [University], which has a large building and a library. It is otherwise not very remarkable, unless it be on account of the beautiful ruins of a great catholic church, which Knox had destroyed at the time of the Reformation.

In the harbour I saw a so-called lifeboat, by which in the

previous year the crew and passengers of a stranded vessel had been rescued in a violent storm. If I am not mistaken, the invention of these boats is due to the French; they have, however, been brought to greater perfection in England, and such boats are now found in all considerable harbours, and even at smaller places, where the entry is difficult. The first lifeboat was built at Shields, near the entry to Newcastle, and in that roadstead, in a few years, 470 persons, who would probably otherwise have been lost, have been rescued. In Newcastle a fine engraving is on sale, which portrays an expedition to a stranded ship, and anyone who has seen the sea in a rage cannot look at this piece without a mixture of horror and admiration. The lifeboat is without a keel, and formed like a segment of an orange; considerably spread out in the middle and pointed at the ends. Usually it is equipped with three pairs of oars, and is steered by means of a movable rudder in the form of a broad spade, which is operated through a loop in the cable fastened to the hull. The manoeuvre with this system of steering is exactly the same as on the river barges in West Bothnia, but because the lifeboat is so arranged that it does not need to be turned, there is such a rudder at the bow and stern, and two steersmen operate them according to the circumstances. In order to give the boat a certain stiffness, instead of a keel two long timbers are fixed along the length somewhat below the scuppers, and the gunwale is clad with cork in the middle in order to carry more, and to moderate the impact on approaching a ship. When such a boat is crewed by experienced seamen, it can neither capsize nor sink in the worst storm. As proof of this I must mention that on one occasion they had forgotten in the hurry to plug a hole in the centre of the boat, through which normally the bilge water runs out when the boat is drawn up on land. Notwithstanding this, several trips were made to a ship before it was discovered.

It is true that the construction of the boats does not allow of a sail; however, I saw at Mr Bigge's in Newcastle the model of a lifeboat with sails, which was to be submitted to the King; this model had three broad beams which were set upright in three holes towards the middle of the boat, and so fitted that they could easily be pushed up and down. It was thought that by pushing the beams down to a certain depth below the bottom, the boat would be given the stability necessary to drive it by sails, and when the beams were raised, it would be operated in the usual manner by rowing.[26]

At St Andrews we left the coast and took our way inland through the town of Cupar to an estate named Lautrisk, the present owner of which, Johnstone, had been a business man in Gothenburg for several years. Near Cupar the countryside already begins to take on a different aspect. Fewer large meadows are to be seen, the hills are more covered with soil, and the flat sandy heaths, which otherwise serve for cattle grazing, are in several places adorned with plantations of pine, spruce, and larch. Some of these plantations, the extent of which, however, was not considerable, could yield ordinary building timber, especially the spruce and larch. Between Cupar and Lautrisk was more coniferous timber than I had seen anywhere else in England and Scotland, and which for the most part had been planted within a space of time from 16 to 20 years. Most of it belonged to Mr Johnstone, whose precinct extends for a few English miles in length and breadth. He had purchased this estate about 16 years before, for £32,000 sterling, and he believed that he could now recover that merely from the timber which he had himself planted, if he cared to cut it all at once. The pine trees had, so it seemed, flourished less well: the larches grew fastest and after these the spruce; in general, however, the growth of the timber was nowhere near as great as in most

L

provinces of Sweden, where they understand the culture of woodland and know its value. Between these parks, especially in the neighbourhood of the house, were tolerable fields and meadows, and on the gentle slope of an elevation, which enclosed part of the plain, there was a quarry, from which was brought material for a large number of farmhouses, which were in part already built, in part in process of building.

Mr Johnstone had recently had built a threshing machine of the kind which is known in Sweden as an English threshing machine. It was built up on a horizontal cog-wheel of 16 to 18 feet diameter, which engaged with a 1 foot diameter gear fastened to the axle of the threshing roller. The diameter of the threshing roll was 4 feet, and two fluted iron rollers, which brought up the unthreshed grain, were each $4\frac{1}{2}$ inches. A cleaning machine below the threshing roll separated the small straw and a part of the chaff, but the winnowing was finally done by hand. With this machine a boll, or rather more than a Swedish ton of corn was threshed in an hour, it being driven by four strong horses. For the threshing which was merely started to show us the machine, only two horses were used, but they had to exert all their strength. When the threshing is in full operation, and four horses are used, they can seldom keep on for longer than six hours a day. It therefore runs harder and produces on the whole less effect than those which have been built in Sweden in recent times. What must be a great relief for the horses is the contrivance with four traction beams on the centre post, in the midst of which they are harnessed, as is the general usage in France and England nowadays.

A few English miles from Lautrisk, towards the sea, lies the Leven ironworks, which belongs to a company which began to work here two years ago. The works already consisted of one blast furnace with two shafts, of which one was in operation; several other workshops for rolling the bar iron, for casting, etc, were partly already begun, partly plannned. The position of the works on a brook, which comes from a fairly large lake, named Loch Leven, had here given the opportunity of maintaining a 20 feet high fall by means of an aqueduct, with which the blast furnace blower was now worked.

The blower was unlike those so far seen in every respect. It consisted of an overshot waterwheel of 20 to 22 feet diameter and five feet wide over the buckets, with a three-throw crank fastened to the centre of the wheel. From each of the three throws of the crank rods went up to one end of three associated beams, from the other ends of which rods were connected vertically with the pistons of three iron cylinders. The blowing pistons therefore received their motion in just the same manner as in the blowers with steam engines, and the crank operated on the opposite end of the beam in the same way as it acts directly on the Widholm bellows. The diameter of the blowers was about 5 feet, and their stroke four feet. The wind was conducted from the three cylinders through pipes into a large cylindrical cast-iron reservoir, the turned movable cover of which was loaded with 3 pounds per square inch. From this a further two pipes went out, one of them straight on to the blast furnace, dividing half-way along into two smaller parallel pipes, through which a part of the wind was led to one long side of the hearth, which here had two tapholes 15 or 16 inches apart. The second pipe, which stood at right angles to the first, conducted another part of the blast around the furnace to the opposite long side of the hearth, where the blast was put in through a single tuyère. The hearth therefore had three tuyères, two of which were set next to one another and the third on the opposite side so that the blast coming in through it played directly between the two first air currents. Otherwise the structure of the blast furnace and hearth was normal. The shaft, 38 feet from the hearthstone to the charging platform, was very narrow towards the top. When the furnace was in full operation, it gave 30 tons of iron weekly. They had not yet had enough experience to judge of the usefulness of this construction, which is regarded by several skilled ironworkers as a mere experiment. In any case they had found the blast to be inadequate for both blast furnace shafts, and they were on this account thinking of connecting a steam engine to it, to strengthen the blast.

The situation of this works seems in many respects to be very advantageous. Almost all the seams, from which the coal and ironstone are brought, lay higher than the charging level of the blast furnace, and most of them only a few hundred yards from it, which gave the opportunity of facilitating the transport of the most important materials by railways in the future; the already built aqueduct saves in part the cost of steam engines, and ensures a comfortable and plentiful water supply, for everything which may yet possibly be installed. The transport by road for a few English miles to the nearest port could indeed make export rather dearer in the beginning, but they could partly count upon many sales on site, and partly there were other ways of easing the export of production. The nearness of the extensive timber plantations could also give rise to several speculations, which could not conveniently happen at other works.

The coal and ironstone seams had not yet been sufficiently explored for a systematic idea of their positions and extent to be formed. The various trial borings which have been made in 18 months, or since the foundation of the works bear witness, however, to rich and plentiful supplies. In one of these bores a 10 foot thick coal seam was encountered at 34 fathoms deep, and a few fathoms deeper another, $8\frac{1}{2}$ feet thick. Here there were, as usually appears

London. The land in this district is hilly and infertile, and round about the works itself one can see, as in Wales, the struggle between a wild Nature and the creative English [Scottish] industry. The first installations of this works, which John Wilson began a few years ago in partnership with his brother William, are said to have cost on completion £100,000 sterling. It consisted at that time of two blast furnaces and several helve hammers constructed according to the old English, or almost the Swedish method, but after John Wilson had become the sole owner of the works and found that this method of refining was not profitable, a part of the old works was pulled down already in 1802 and in its place the installation of puddling furnaces and rolling mills for an annual production of 1,500 tons of bar iron was begun. During this not yet completed building work, they had collected a supply of 1,400 tons of pig iron besides a quantity of castings, among which were flywheels and other pieces of 7 to 8 tons weight, for the requirements of this works. A tourist cannot expect straight answers to improper questions, so I could not ask to be told the cost of this alteration, but from the knowledge which I believe I have of the expenses of this kind of work, I would hazard the guess that before it is all in working order, the costs may run to £30,000 or more. Although there are plentiful supplies of coal and ore here, and the transport of these materials can also be arranged more easily in time, it yet seems inconceivable how this works, which must take its iron more than two miles overland to the nearest port, can yield a return on the capital invested. However, Mr Wilson is a good patriot, and has sufficient steadfastness to follow a plan which, without paying in the first years, gives an almost certain hope of high returns for the future, and through which in any case a place of refuge is prepared for many people who, otherwise than in wartime, would have to seek their living in foreign parts.

The coal and ironstone seams, which, with the usual compression by intrusive dykes, extend over a mile from the works, were recently explored by drilling, and found to be more than sufficient for the new plant. The most substantial of the coal seams now worked lay 19 fathoms deep and was rather more than 4 feet thick. The ironstone occurred alternately above and below the coal, either in so-called bands or deposits or in the form of the above-mentioned balls. The latter sometimes lay immediately below the topsoil, and were unusually large, weighing up to 1 ton or more.

The seams were covered on top, beneath the surface soil, more or less deeply with peat, which was now, where the drainage of water had been brought about by nature or by art, completely dried out. In other places it formed ordinary peat bogs, enclosed by chalk and sandstone hills. There was such a bog above the works, which was already partially dried out by boring. This boring is done in the following manner: in the dry seasons the dampest spots are sought out, where the spring of the water can be clearly noticed. In the slope below and near to such a spot, holes are bored with a drill two to three fathoms deep, at which depth the underground watercourse is generally encountered, which then rapidly spurts out like a fountain. From here the water is led into one of the main ponds, and then farther, into the works. The present manager of the work, Mr William Wilson, had taken up this work with enthusiasm, and had already got so far with it, that in the previous year (1802) he was able to plant 100,000 pine, spruce, and larch trees on this peat bog, and at the same time had provided a new water supply for the steam engines. His intention was to carry on the planting of timber already begun, in other places, in which he seemed to have an interest which proved that he knew the value of timber, and in this, as in all else did not calculate merely for the present. One must certainly sincerely wish Mr Wilson good luck with his gallant undertaking; yet the secret thought arose within me that he would never be able to burn a charcoal pile on this woodland, because the condition of the soil and the lack of protection for the young saplings must place insurmountable obstacles in the way of their vigorous growth for many years. The advantage would probably have been more certain, if they had converted the bog into field and meadows by draining the water and by fertilising with lime, as has already been started in some places.

A few English miles from Wilsontown, at [New] Lanark, we looked at a large cotton spinning mill, which had been founded a few years before by a business man in Glasgow, but which had now been sold to a London company for £84,000 sterling. It consisted of four buildings several storeys high merely for carding or combing and spinning the cotton, as well as a number of workshops and small houses for the workers. Because the place was almost uninhabited at the foundation of the works, they had here been able without particular expense to observe a certain symmetry, and to give the buildings an appearance which is usually missing from English factories. This, and the fine situation on the bank of the River Clyde below the famous waterfall, made the place into one of the most beautiful and interesting of the whole district.

At each of the above-mentioned four spinning mills was a low overshot water wheel a few feet wide, which drove the whole of the machinery, which was made entirely of cast iron, from the largest to the smallest hand-wheels. The head for the wheel was obtained from the River Clyde by means of a waterway which went for almost an English mile, partially underground. In one of the large halls, where the spinning was completed, 2,060 threads were spun at once. In each hall they reckon in general on four hundredweights per week of moderately fine cotton yarn, and less of the finest. A part of the works was now being overhauled, and it was said that the weekly production did not exceed nine hundredweights in total. If one assumes that normally this is only ten hundredweights, and reckons 50 working weeks to the year, there nevertheless results a production of 500 hundredweights annually. The cotton worked here therefore amounts to nearly one-sixth of the bar iron which is forged at a two-hearth hammer in Sweden. I should remark in this connection that although this mill is one of the largest in the Kingdom, there are proportionately many more smaller ones, especially around Glasgow, Liverpool, and in Manchester, and I should imagine that the output of cotton yarn in and in the neighbourhood of these towns almost equals the weight of copper production at Fahlun.

From Lanark the route went to the little town of Hamilton, where we spent the night, and in the neighbourhood of which on the following day we inspected a well-furnished but old and dark castle of the Duke of Hamilton.

The stretch of country between Wilsontown and Clyde was more beautiful and more cultivated than that between the first-named place and Edinburgh. The ground was fairly level, but in the distance there showed the high mountain ranges which occur in certain parts of Lanarkshire, especially in the neighbourhood of the large lead works at Leadhills.

The Clyde ironworks, named after the river of that name which flows past it, lies only a few English miles from Glasgow. It belongs to a company, and is now under the supervision of a Mr Outram from Derbyshire. Next to Carron, Clyde is the largest ironfoundry in Scotland, and consists of three blast furnaces, various air furnaces and cupolas. No wrought iron is made here, but good cannon and all sorts of fine and rough castings are poured.

The blower for all three blast furnaces was driven by a steam engine of 55 horsepower. There was nothing special about it apart from a regulator, which consisted of three large iron cylinders, which stood in a tank of water a few feet high. Into these cylinders, in which at any time, when the blower stopped, the water stood at a certain height, the wind was led through iron pipes from the large blowing cylinder, so that the air emerged somewhat above the surface of the water. Afterwards the blast was taken through another opening in each of the inverted cylinders, into the blast furnaces by means of iron pipes, and the water, which was here pushed out of the cylinders by each stroke of the piston, and immediately rose in the tank, therefore served by its counterweight to maintain an even blast.

The most recently built blast furnace, which was 38 feet high from the hearthstone to the charging platform, 3 feet wide at the crown, 11 feet 9 inches at the bosh, and 2 feet 6 inches at the hearth band (end of the well, which took up 8 feet above the hearthstone), was lined on the inside with refractory bricks, and separated by an evacuated space from the outer wall (the smoke wall). The latter takes up a 30 foot square at the foundations, but higher up it was rounded off, so that at the crown the entire structure formed a perfect cylinder of 12 feet diameter. The outside, like the hearth, was entirely of dressed stone. A more exact description of the blast furnaces here, the size of the charges, etc. will be given on a future occasion, and I content myself here merely with remarking that in order to get the best kind of grey cast iron for cannon, the weekly output is seldom taken higher than 25 tons, that is, a little more than the quantity at which individual Swedish blast furnaces are overworked. Since Mr Garney's many years of experience would have been no more able than the constant complaints of the forgemaster to convince the majority of the Swedish ironmasters of the precarious profitability of an excessive weekly output under certain circumstances, I would wish that at least the experience of the English, which has been several times noted in this respect, might give rise to the investigation of this part of the art so important to all pig-iron production.

Near the works are a few coal mines, wherein ironstone likewise occurs; most of it was won, however, at a place named Crosbasket [Crossbasket], 3 to 4 English miles distant. This ore sometimes occurs in so-called bands, occasionally one foot thick. In one of these seams thirty such deposits, one over the other, have been counted in a fairly large area, so that supplies of both coal and ironstone are here regarded as inexhaustible. Near these ironstone deposits several coal mines are worked, from which the surrounding villages are provided with fuel; between the coal occur various kinds of clay, shale, and chalk, with or without fossils. Beneath the ironstone deposits sandstone of several varieties is encountered. For certain castings a rich red haematite from Cumberland is added.

The boring of the cannon is done here, as everywhere in England, in the horizontal position. The boring and turning machine was driven by a steam engine, and four cannon could be turned and bored at once. The turning was done by hand, often by boys, and just as easily as turning a piece of wood. The cast iron was unusually strong and dense, but on the other hand so soft that it could almost be filed like wrought iron.

For drilling the touch-hole Mr Outram had invented a small machine, concerning which he intended to apply for a patent. This machine could be moved quickly from one cannon to another by one workman, and by its means the touch-hole could be given exactly any desired position and size in two or three minutes; it was however, assembled in such a fashion that no description of it can be given here.

For transporting small cannon from one place to another,

Mr Outram had likewise devised a truck, which deserves mention on account of its great simplicity. It had wheels 5 feet high, which ran on an iron axle as in ordinary trucks, and above this axle was a strong iron arch, three-quarters of a yard high, in the centre of which was fixed a wooden draw-shaft which extended $1\frac{1}{4}$ yards behind the arch, above which it was curved to either side, so that the ends of the curves in this length met somewhat above the centrepoint of the wheels, from which they then went out straight, like a normal shaft. At each end of this curve strong iron nails were driven in, to which iron chains were fixed in such a manner that when they were hooked on at both ends and the shaft stood horizontal, they hung about a foot above the ground. When a cannon was to be moved, the truck was placed in such a direction that the cranked part of the shaft was exactly parallel with the position of the cannon, whereupon one of the workmen lifted the shaft high enough so that the rear chain touched the ground, and could therefore easily be placed under one end of the cannon by another worker. Then the shaft was depressed and the forward chain brought in just the same way under the other end of the cannon, which now hung centrally under the axle, about 10 to 12 inches from the ground. With this machine two strong people took several six-pounder cannons to the boring machine in a short time and over a fairly uneven path.

In the foundry several 10 to 12 year old boys were employed, who moulded small pans and other fine castings in sand with admirable skill. One of the lads pushed his daily wages higher than one of the older moulders was able to do.

Before I leave Clyde, I must mention the famous Mushet [David Mushet, 1772-1847], who at the time when he began his experiments and wrote the first treatise on iron [A dozen or so separate papers, published originally in the

Philosophical Magazine between 1798 and the time of Svedenstierna's tour, and brought together in a collected edition as *Papers on Iron and Steel* (London, 1840)], was employed at the foundry here. Without any knowledge of chemistry or any other studies, he had, as a junior labourer at the works, already begun to make several observations about the melting and the behaviour of the cast iron, concerning which he could not get satisfaction from any of the available writings. He accordingly decided to study chemistry himself, and attended, as often as his time allowed, the chemical lectures at Glasgow. His inclination to science grew in proportion to the light which it shed on the operations which he saw daily on a large scale, and some fortunate experiments, as well as the above-mentioned treatise, aroused such confidence in him, that he was soon given the supervision of the works. Because he thereby received a free hand to put his theories of iron into practice to a great measure, he was thus perhaps led to go further than economic caution allowed. Several persons worthy of belief even told me that during his management worse iron, and at a higher cost, was made at the Clyde Ironworks than at any other works in Scotland. Mushet was therefore dismissed, and now he joined with some capitalists and business men in Glasgow in the Calder Ironworks, nearer to Edinburgh. Here he enthusiastically gave precedence to his experiments, which he continued to make known in Tilloch's *Philosophical Magazine*; he was, however, so unfortunate in the management of the works that in three years he had not only caused his fellow-investors a loss of several thousand pounds, but also lost his own small means. The works was now shut down and put up for sale and the affairs of the company were in chancery. Everywhere there are people who know neither how to praise nor to blame, and thus it comes about that Mushet is decried by some as a charlatan, and looked upon by others as an oracle. His enemies would even deny him the merit of being the author of his own writings, which they ascribe to his wife. Even if this were true, it would do great credit to the education of Scottish ladies, without in the least detracting from the value of Mushet's experiments and observations; for these reveal a penetration, a method, and a real knowledge of iron, which is to be found in few authors who have contributed to the explanation of the nature of this so generally used, but so little understood metal. The usual imprudence of drawing general conclusions from a few simple facts, and the too-audacious application of a theory not yet properly established, are the errors of which one can justly accuse Mushet. But nothing can prove his love of the truth better than this: that he has already realised and corrected several errors, and this, in a land where this is as easily excused as deliberate deception is never forgiven, cannot fail to ensure that he will once again be helped and again set on the way to serve the public with his discoveries, and perhaps principally with his dearly bought experience in economics.

It is far from my intention here completely to excuse Mushet, for it is and always will be a great fault not to calculate the cost of an undertaking the principal object of which is to earn money, and in an unwise zeal for a science to destroy his own fortune and those of others; but I do not wish to see a man of distinguished merit in certain respects, and of otherwise unimpeachable behaviour, counted among the real charlatans, who are to be found in every country and who, without knowledge and experience, partly out of discontent, partly out of desire to make their fortunes, try again and again to overturn everything old, and by a voice suited to the circumstances, by a certain suppleness in mixing with people, know how to obtain patrons and followers, who finally are in part enlightened by their losses, but who can seldom distinguish the mistakes of a truly scientifically educated man from the gross errors of untrained imitators.

With these considerations, which presented rich material for the annoyance of my travelling companion concerning the loss of some thousands of pounds which one of his friends had suffered in the Calder company, we left Clyde and arrived at Glasgow. The short stay in this town did not allow me to see and to get to know the many excellent works and factories which are situated here and in the neighbourhood, among which are various large cotton spinning mills, muslin and calico factories, dyeworks, etc.

In a factory belonging to one Mr Macintosh, a beautiful red dye was made from the Bohusland mountain lichen, which people in Sweden have already attempted to refine, but without making progress. I do not know whether lack of knowledge on the part of the manufacturers, or lack of sales, was to blame for this.

A recently founded factory, in which 150 workers were engaged daily in the finishing of genuine porcelain, with earthenware according to Wedgwood's invention, and other coarser kinds, deserves much attention. One finds there collected together several of the inventions which I have seen individually at other porcelain factories in England and France.

A device in finishing fine muslin, which I accidentally managed to see in Glasgow, must here be mentioned, at least on account of its curiosity. The purpose of it was presumably to remove all the fluff and little pills which arise on the surface of the muslin in weaving. This purpose was served by a brick-built furnace 4 to 5 feet high, into which was fitted, along the length of the hearth, a cylinder of cast iron of 12 to 13 inches diameter and a few feet long, in such a manner that two-thirds of its volume lay above the wall. On either side of the furnace were two rollers with cranks, and in the centre above the cylinder an easily movable rod was fixed beneath the roof. When the cylinder was completely red-hot, a piece of stuff was wound upon one of the rollers, pulled over the rod, and fastened to the empty roller. Then one workman stationed himself at each handle, and the third in the centre before the rod, which at a given signal was pulled out, whereupon the material at once fell on to the hot cylinder, and was pulled over it by constant rotation of the rollers, until the entire piece of muslin was wound on to the roller which was empty at the start of the operation.

It is easy to see that a correctly gauged speed and an even movement is the main thing here, for if the fine muslin touches the iron cylinder only one or two seconds longer than it has to, it would certainly burst into flames. I later saw the same device used in Manchester with velveteen, and I rather believe that it can with advantage be used in finishing several textiles.

Glasgow has a very fine situation between the River Clyde and the Monkland canal, which latter forms a branch of the Forth & Clyde canal. Only small vessels can come up to the town. The harbour itself is therefore two or three Swedish miles away, at a place called Port Glasgow. Trade has greatly extended here in the last few years, to which the new canal has certainly contributed, although people complain that voyages through it progress slowly, that the canal is too large for small barges and too small for ships, and that the installations do not entirely answer their purpose. It is somewhat narrower than the Trollhätta canal, and about the same depth.

Glasgow is not so well built as the new town of Edinburgh, but better than the old, and one finds here fine massive buildings, among which the military hospital and the new theatre are especially distinguished. Although the harbour is farther away from here than is Leith from Edinburgh, the commerce is more active on account of the many factories. Also in recent years large amounts of capital have settled in Glasgow, of which a part, however, has moved to Edinburgh, where there are more amusements, and the manner of life is in general more brilliant. The Scots are therefore accustomed to say that one earns money in Glasgow and spends it in Edinburgh.

In the neighbourhood of Glasgow, especially at Paisley, are rich coalmines which are intensively worked, and whose haulage machines seem to be very complete.

A little way from the town lies the Hurlet alum and vitriol works which belongs to a Mr Macintosh. The alum occurs here mainly as exudations from the shale in old coalmines or on the neighbouring slag-heaps. The process is therefore very simple, and consists merely of the extraction and boiling of the shale with the addition of sulphuric acidulated soda [sodium hydrogen sulphate]. This salt is obtained in great quantities from the works where bleaching is done with dephlogisticated spirits of salts [chlorine] and in the soap works from the residue after the extraction of barilla, on which account it can be had at a very low price, as it is otherwise of little use. After the appropriate boiling the lye is run into large butts, wherein it is left for two or three weeks to crystallise. This crystallisation begins on the surface, around the edges and on the bottom, and continues up to the centre, where the mother liquor finally remains. When it is assumed that crystallisation has ceased, the hoops are knocked off the casks and an opening made in the great alum mass, through which most of the mother liquor runs out. The mass is then broken in pieces, and when these have dried out for a time, packed for sale in casks. This, like all the other English alum which I have seen, is neither so clear nor so free from foreign matter as that from the Garphütte in Sweden; it is, however, usually sold in France about 10 per cent dearer than the Swedish, and is very much sought after in Paris for preparing the colours in dyeworks and cordova leather factories. A very skilled druggist in Paris also declared, that the English alum is stronger, although he admitted that the Swedish is more pure and better adapted for some purposes. Because, however, he could not explain to me what he understood by 'stronger' alum, I must almost believe that it is mixed with some kind of foreign matter, and that it is the same with alum as with cooking salt, which is considered as more valuable at the saltworks, according to the degree of im-purity through calcium chloride or magnesia.

When one knows how abundantly natural alum occurs in some countries almost pure and in others mixed with substances from which it can be separated by a very simple procedure, it is almost inconceivable how an alum works could in recent years be founded and operated with profit in South France, where clay is first impregnated with sulphur vapour, and the alum thus produced afterwards extracted. I do not know whether this works, which was founded by the Minister Chaptal, when he was still a professor at Montpellier, is still in operation; at least this seems impossible without the strictest application of the prohibition system, through which factories little suited to a country can be made supportable for single individuals, although it can never be of advantage to the public to bring forth, so to speak, new branches which in their nature can have no certain growth.

For extracting the alum shale at Hurlet an apparatus was made according to the Rumford principles, that is, to heat the water by steam. This consisted of a large steam boiler of iron plates, like the ordinary boilers on the steam engines, from which the hot steam was led through pipes into tanks built of squared stone, and of several thousand gallons capacity. These latter, filled with cold water, could be brought to the boil in two hours. It is easy to see how much such an installation must contribute to the saving of heating vessels and to ease of layout of a works where a large quantity of boiling water is required, to say nothing of the fact that a mass of water is heated more quickly in this way than with normal heating arrangements. This method of heating has now also been taken up in England at various breweries, dyeworks, hatters, and several other factories, and might well be adopted with advantage by us. Mr Macintosh had admittedly found no saving in fuel with it; however, when it is remembered what a loss of heat must arise from the fact that the tanks were here of stone and set deeply into the ground, it is credible that the expenditure on fuel is substantially reduced, when the boiling is done in wooden vessels. Another circumstance, that the water cannot without difficulty be brought to a temperature of a full 100 degrees, could be a disadvantage in certain cases; but a higher temperature could, if it were necessary, certainly be obtained by insulating the pipes with some rough woollen cloth or the like. The water in the boiler, which is constantly reduced, must be replaced through an inlet pipe of a suitable size; likewise it must be reckoned that the condensed steam will increase the quantity of water in the tanks in a certain proportion. It is therefore clear, that this method cannot be used for evaporation or boiling down.

The vitriol works was arranged in the same simple fashion as the one at Newcastle already described, and the production could be expanded in proportion to the sales.

Near Hurlet are several old coalmines, whose seams probably have some relationship with those around Paisley, on which considerable work has been done in more recent times. On either side of the way from here to Kilmarnock, a small town 3 to 4 Swedish miles from Glasgow, large plains could be seen, which consisted mainly of peat bogs, and were little or not at all cultivated. The district here has in general a poor appearance. In a little inn, where we changed horses, a kind of coarse oat bread was baked, which was like the thin corn bread of West Bothnia. The method of doing it was very simple. After a piece of dough was rolled out to the breadth and thickness of a strong sheet of paper, it was laid for a few minutes on an iron plate over the ordinary kitchen fire, which was here fed partly with peat and partly with balls of small coal and mud.[27]

On departing from Kilmarnock we made a detour to Douglas Castle, an old knightly seat, on whose territories were some chalk quarries and coalmines, which were not very highly worked. Towards evening we came to Old Cumnock, a little village between Kilmarnock and Sanquhar. The countryside was here better cultivated, and in certain places wooded with deciduous timber.

A bare Swedish mile from Old Cumnock there is a graphite mine, belonging to a Mr Taylor. This was started up a few years ago, but had now been closed down for some time on account of lack of sales. From the village up to the mine the land rises, takes on a wild appearance, and is only inhabited by a few farmers, whose principal livelihood is cattle grazing. However, Mr Taylor told us that one of these farmers, who we visited on the return journey, paid £500 sterling annually for his grazing land, even though, to judge by his dwelling, one would rather have taken him for a poor squatter. The moors and valleys here, which on one side stretch to the horizon, and on the others are enclosed by a high country, are actually chalk and sedimentary rocks covered with soil. In one of the latter the graphite mine is driven a few fathoms deep, according to the inclination of the strata, which here varies over short distances, but in general is more pronounced than usual. At the entrance to the mine, where the rocks were cut through vertically about 3 fathoms deep from the surface, the strata seemed to consist of the following types of stone.

Immediately under the surface soil, a thin layer of a kind of shale; after that a thicker one of fine hard sandstone, beneath which was a still denser quartz rock, cut through by fine cracks, which is named lava according to Hutton's system, but which is less glassy, and rather resembles the sandstone from old blast furnace hearths. Below that lay the seam of graphite, which is a few feet thick, and obvious on the surface merely through a few small sparks or veins, compressed in a glass-like quartz rock; farther on it showed itself in larger masses, which, so to speak, made up a cover or a bed for the last-mentioned type of rock; the latter then took the form of nodules, which often have a diameter of some feet. These nodules vanished farther down in the depths, and with them the graphite, which changed stepwise into coke or carbonised coal, which over a small distance took up the entire thickness of the seam, but afterwards was changed successively into ordinary coal, in which the mine, so far as it was open, was sunk. Below the last mentioned seam occurred a kind of coarse-grained hornstone, and below that, again sandstone.

How the transition described here from coal into coke and from that into graphite, like the vitrification of the quartz material, can have taken place without the effect of subterranean fire, is difficult to conceive. Mr Jameson of Edinburgh, who has closely investigated this seam, seems, however, to have an idea, and he promised shortly to announce something about it in print. The best graphite here approaches very closely in quality to that of Keswick in Cumberland, which is considered to be the finest, and for a pound of which $2\frac{1}{2}$ to 3 guineas is paid in London. Mr Taylor intends to use the less good kinds in a recently founded factory for crucibles and fireproof bricks, for which he promised many advantages.

On the road from Old Cumnock to the town of Sanquhar we left the Muirkirk ironworks behind on the left. It

161

M*

consists of three blast furnaces and some other workshops, and is now operated by a company.

The district here seemed to be moderately cultivated, in some places thinly clad with deciduous trees, and generally hilly and cut through by little streams. At one of these latter, a few English miles from Cumnock, we found in soft deposits a beautiful jasper of various colours, which occurs in several places in Scotland, likewise a chalcedon coloured edged pebble, from which seals, medallions for necklaces and the like are cut, and which, under the name of Scotch Pebbles are sold in every jewellers shop in England. Near to Sanquhar a few coalmines were worked, and 6 to 7 Swedish quarter-miles to the north lies Leadhills, where there are rich lead mines and smelting works. The annual production of these is said to amount to about 1,000 tons.

As soon as one is past Sanquhar the district takes on a pleasanter appearance, and is more cultivated and built up, the nearer one gets to the town of Dumfries. The houses here are generally built of a red sandstone, which is rather darker than that of Orsa in Dalarna. Where this type of stone begins to show itself, the coal seams cease, which is supposed to be the case in the whole of Scotland.

A few English miles from Dumfries lies one of the most beautiful estates in Scotland, which belongs to a Mr Miller, who we visited in passing. He appeared now to be a man of about fifty years, and had already been engaged for twenty years with a new construction of ships, which would be able to continue their course in a calm as well as in unfavourable winds. These ships, one of which Mr Miller presented to King Gustav III, are equipped with two keels, between which are fixed wheels, through which the ship is supposed to be moved by a force independent of wind and weather. It is said that Miller has expended nearly £20,000 sterling upon his experiments in this case, and although neither the English nor the Swedish Admiralty has found his construction to be good and acceptable, he is yet convinced that nothing but an old prejudice is to blame for this. On a small lake which adjoins his estate, we saw a little flotilla of sloops and boats with double keels. Miller, whose fortune is estimated at £60,000 to £70,000 sterling, is, however, a clever and estimable man, who always works at his own expense, and thereby significantly distinguishes himself from the bulk of inventors and creators of the unusable.

Dumfries is a fairly large town, mostly built of the above-mentioned red sandstone. Immediately before the town on the way to Carlisle begin great plains, which extend for 3 to 4 Swedish miles long up to Gretna Green on the English border. These plains consist for the most part of dried-up peat bogs, which often rise two to three feet above the highway. In some places, where peat was cut for fuel, it was possible to work down 5 feet into the bog with terraces (benches), without being specially inconvenienced by water. The best peat consisted here of a fine cohesive sludge, very similar to the Dutch peat or that which occurs in certain parts of West Gotland. Long stretches of these bogs were already cultivated, and promised a rich harvest of various kinds of grain and grass; others were now being brought into cultivation, which was begun by draining the terrain in longish rectangles and by the application of burnt lime; the latter was so heavily applied in some places that the soil was completely covered by it. It is difficult for a traveller to see who looks after this cultivation, since one often encounters merely a few small miserable houses over a whole Swedish mile. As soon as one has passed the little stream at Gretna Green, which divides Scotland from England, the country becomes less low-lying and is adorned here and there, especially in the neighbourhood of Carlisle, with beautiful timber plantations.

Chapter 7

The North-West

THE LATTER TOWN [CARLISLE], WHICH LIES NEAR TO THE border, is one of the oldest in the country, more badly than well built, with long crooked alleys, but in a fine situation. The houses are built partly of the above-mentioned red standstone, partly of bricks, which are here made in great quantities near to the town. Among the manufactures of the town the making of fish-hooks is the most remarkable. These latter are made here in greater quantities and better than anywhere else in England.

From Carlisle to the lead mines at Aldstone [Alston] Moor, where we wanted to go, there are two ways, one of about 4 and the other nearly 6 Swedish miles. Because it is difficult to get horses on the first route, we were advised to take the other way through the town of Penrith, from whence it is about $3\frac{1}{2}$ Swedish miles to Aldstone Moor. On arrival in Penrith, no one would drive us without four horses to a post-chaise. We had to spend at least three days at Aldstone Moor, and, because a post-chaise was not obtainable there, we should have had to have kept the present one with us, and paid the expenses of the coachman and the horses. On a careful calculation the costs of this ran to £9 sterling, so we decided to go on foot, and only to take with us a horse to carry the necessary articles and a man as guide. Anyone whose health and strength do not permit of the journey on foot, and who perhaps has less time than we had, can make just this journey in comfort and with little cost, if he books a seat in one of the public coaches which go two or three times weekly between Carlisle and Newcastle, to Hexam [Hexham] from where there is a public road to Aldstone Moor, five Swedish quarter miles at the most. I introduce this here, partly for the information of future tourists, who could possibly make this tour, partly as a proof of the usefulness of being acquainted with the map, if one leaves the larger highways in England. This is especially necessary if one journeys in certain parts of Devonshire, Cornwall, Wales, Westmoreland, Cumberland, Yorkshire, and Northumberland, where the districts are very hilly, and where in many places there are no or anyway very bad roads.

At the distance of a Swedish mile from Carlisle the land already begins to get higher. On the extensive fields and heaths up to Penrith, there are few houses, no cultivated fields or meadows, but merely a few scattered cattle grazings. Around Penrith was some cultivated land, but as soon as one is a few English miles past the town, there is a completely desolate district, which extends for about $1\frac{1}{2}$ Swedish miles up to Aldstone Moor. On the slopes of the mountain ridge. which here parts the water to east and west, we saw several coal seams on the surface, which, however, are worked only for the household requirements of the villages in the valley. This ridge rises fairly steeply, and forms a hill about half a Swedish mile long, down to the road. Also from the ridge there is a wide view on one side over the town of Penrith and the surrounding fields as far as the bare and pointed mountains near Keswick, and on another side to the rounded summits which formed a continuation of the height on which we stood; some of these summits are so high that they were still partially covered with snow at the beginning of June. All these mountains are either sedimentary, or if they contain no ordered strata, they yet consist of almost the same rock types which occur in and around sedimentary mountains, so that neither granite, gneiss, nor other primordial rocks are found here.

No trees occur on any of these mountains, notwithstanding that they are all covered to a substantial depth with soil and gravel. What particularly struck me was that on every mountain summit which we scaled, we encountered marshy ground full of springs of water, but on the other hand neither a pool nor a peat bog in the tiniest depressions. The Tyne and Wear rise on this stretch of mountains, from which the former runs into the sea near Shields below Newcastle and the latter at Sunderland. When one descends from the above-mentioned height, one has a free view over the valley in which the Tyne meanders, to the high mountains on the borders of Cumberland, Durham, and Northumberland, which for the most part contain rich deposits of lead ore.

Aldstone Moor lies in a valley—a small and badly built town, inhabited mainly by miners and other workers employed in the lead smelting works. The mines, founded near the town over a stretch of 3 to 4 Swedish quartermiles, are now operated by various companies, who either work the lodes and ore deposits already revealed, on payment of a consideration to the landowner, or are permitted to seek for similar ones in a certain field. Usually the deposits are opened up by the landowner by means of galleries, and then leased out to the highest bidder. The Hospital at Greenwich, which possesses the landlord's rights of a large tract near to the town, has in this way created a large income for itself from several mines now in operation, and work was now proceeding on an exploratory gallery, which was said to stretch for several hundred fathoms into one of the most important minefields. This gallery, which already passes twice beneath the bed of the River Tyne, was so arranged that the water therein was always maintained at a given level, and thus ore and rubble could be transported on barges, as is the case on the canals in some coalmines mentioned earlier.

The ore here consists mainly of galena, with some admixture of a greyish ochre (Plomb Oxide terreux Hauy), and some little carbonated lead, which, however, occurs mostly in fine needle-like crystals. In some mines one finds unusual mixtures of lead ochre, oxidised zinc, and manganese, the use of which had not yet been considered. In the ore deposits there are several fine variations of fluorspar in crystals, chalk, carbonated and sulphated baryta [barium carbonate and barium sulphate], as well as less common fossils. The rock types which could be investigated, partly in strata in the larger mines, partly in the sections which the River Tyne presented in several places, were quite unlike those which I had seen earlier, and seemed to me, so far as one could judge by outward appearance, to consist of chalk, sandstone, and baryta mixed intimately and in unequal proportions, so that now one, now another kind was predominant therein. That these types of rock occur in strata and deposits is demonstrated clearly in the abovementioned sections on the banks of the Tyne; but whether the ore has a horizontal position, or whether the seams cut through, so to say, as lodes, I was unable to investigate because of my short stay in the place.

When the ore was brought to the surface either through a gallery or through the shafts sunk here and there on account of change of weather, it was broken into small pieces and levigated or washed. In this work much was discarded which with less rich reserves would certainly have been turned to account, and in the washing or settling, which was done on the bare ground between tiny embanked dykes of the mine water, a large part of the abovementioned lead ochre was lost. The ore was then taken to the smelting works, and here put, together with coal, into a hearth 15 to 18 inches deep, the blower for which consisted of two small leather bellows. In such a hearth 40 to 50 discs or about 20 shippounds of pure lead is made in 24 hours. In smelting down in such a low hearth much lead must necessarily evaporate, and it has therefore been decided to install a smoke trap at one smelting works, less, however, to save lead than to avoid the inconvenience of the fumes for the workmen, who seldom survive at this work for three or four years, and who all looked very sickly. The annual production of the smelting works here, and those at Allenshead, two miles away, is calculated at about 4,000 tons, and in view of the supplies of ore it could have been brought much higher, only in latter years there had been a lack of sales, and the intention was therefore rather to reduce than to increase the production.

From Aldstone Moor our way went back through Penrith, to the little town of Keswick, in the neighbourhood of which lies the famous graphite mine, which belongs to the Hospital of Greenwich. So that the graphite does not fall to too low a price, the mine is only staffed and worked every seventh year, and was now closed down. The district here is much visited by English people on account of its beautiful and romantic appearance, but some lakes here, of which so much is made in England because they are the only ones in the country, are not interesting to a Swede, because he is accustomed to encountering larger ones, with more beautiful shores and with wooded islands, in his native land. On the other hand the mountains here have a quite unusual appearance. Sometimes they rise quite gently, and are then more or less covered with soil; sometimes, however, they tower up quite steeply like a wall several hundred yards high, and culminate in high sharp summits like extinct volcanoes or like a part of the Swedish fjäll mountains.

A basalt more or less mixed with other kinds of rock

appears to make up the principal constituent of the high and steep mountains; but at the foot of these one finds mostly deposits of sandstone, chalk, and several sediments.

On the way from here down into Lancashire the land maintains the same appearance over a distance of some miles, but gradually descends when one comes into Westmoreland, and after that up to Liverpool is for the most part flat. In proportion to this the district becomes also more populous and cultivated, traversed by canals, and has several manufacturing towns, amongst which Lancaster and Preston are the most considerable. Between the latter place and Liverpool one passes several fine estates with the cottagers belonging to them, which latter consist of day-labourers of all kinds, who pay the landlord only an insignificant rent. These cottages usually consist of a little house with kitchen and bedroom, of just the same kind as our smaller day labourer's cottages, and are all built of wattle daubing with or without timbering. The former are considered to be more durable, if they are erected at a suitable time of year, properly plastered, and kept in repair. The method of construction is almost the same as has been introduced for such in recent times in Sweden; the walls are made 21 inches thick at the foot and 12 to 13 at the roof. A Mr Bourne, a business man in Liverpool, who had substantial estates here and in Cheshire, assured me that he had in both places mud houses which stood for 60 to 70 years, without noticeable damage. He added that this method of construction had been tried out on a large scale in several places, which however, was not a success, because the thick walls which were found necessary for a larger building could not be dried in the first summer.

Liverpool, which is now regarded as the largest commercial town in Great Britain after London, is probably, in respect of its extent and population, one of the most important in the whole world. Its commerce has in a space of

15 to 20 years so noticeably increased that whereas Bristol, whose trade may be somewhat in decline, formerly had twice as much commerce as Liverpool, the proportions are now said to be reversed. This is attributed in part to the position, which is very advantageous for overseas trade, for communications with Ireland, and for the commission and transportation business with the large inland manufacturing towns; and in part it is seen as a consequence of the generally recognised industry, mode of living, and thrift of the inhabitants. The harbour here, which is good in itself, has been made more convenient in recent times by means of docks and landing stages, and one needs only to be there for a short time to get an approximate idea of the quantity of goods loaded and unloaded, of the numbers of arriving and departing ships, and of the value of the enormous stocks which are in the warehouse near the harbour.

Already the West Indian trade, in which Liverpool competes even with London, may well demand an unbelievably large capital; for besides seventy or more slave ships, which are annually sent to the African coast, and afterwards take rich cargoes to the West Indies, several small vessels are engaged in this trade. Also I saw here cotton, coffee, and sugar being unloaded in the same quantities as are hemp, flour, and salt in several not so very insignificant Baltic ports. The war declared a few days before had, instead of retarding the commerce, as was generally believed on the continent, made it livelier, at least for a time. During the negotiations no safe speculation could be made; now, however, people had learnt by experience gained in the last war to take precautions, and this had already taught that if one must as a human being sigh over the misfortune of war, the business man can be very satisfied with the capital which the war brings in. Among the ventures which engaged the inhabitants of Liverpool at this moment was particularly the equipping of privateering vessels, which

was done with such a rapidity that five were already fit
for sea before the declaration of war came here, and in
eight days afterwards fifteen others were fitting out, most
of which returned from a short cruise with rich Dutch and
French prizes. Also all the slave ships present, of 16 to 18
guns, were said to have made a cruise before their departure to Africa.

I must take this opportunity to put in something about
the slave trade. One can justly reproach the inhabitants of
Liverpool with the unrighteous support of this iniquitous
traffic, but, as long as it is not abolished throughout the
world, then I believe that it is to a degree better in the
hands of the English than with other nations. At least the
English government has done everything possible to lighten
the fate of the slaves; also the slave traders themselves are
convinced of the advantages of gentle treatment of the
slaves. The English slave ships are commodious and comfortably equipped, and intended for a definite number of
slaves, which may not be exceeded under pain of a very
heavy fine. On each ship there are two doctors, who, besides
their salaries receive a special bonus for each slave who
comes healthy to the market place; it is therefore in their
interest to tend the sick carefully, and to see to it that the
healthy get sufficient nourishment and liberty. This regula-
tion is often missing on the Dutch and French ships, and
the cruel and inhuman treatment of the slaves on these has
sometimes recently led to violent revolts, which, however,
seldom or never happen on the English ships.[28]

In the foregoing something has already been said of the
scientific institutions of London and other English towns:
to which I can now add something in respect of Liverpool.
Already several years ago some business people and persons
of rank had agreed upon the establishment of a literary
society on approximately the same plan as that at Newcastle. To that end a subscription was opened, in which

within a short time 500 persons with 20 guineas each had joined for the first foundation of the institution; besides that every interested person advanced another two guineas annually for the upkeep of the institute and the purchase of new books. Scarcely was this subscription closed, than several people already appeared, who wished to become members of the society, but because space and comfort did not allow of an increase in the number of members, a speculative dealing in the shares resulted, and within four years these rose to 45 guineas. In this space of time some of the sellers as well as several who found this establishment inadequate on account of the crowd of readers, had given consideration to a new one. A fresh subscription was therefore opened, and within three years an elegant and practical house was already erected, which cost rather more than £7,000 sterling. As the institution now stood, almost £11,000 had been spent upon it, including the purchase of the books; however, the society, now consisting of 800 shareholders, each of whom had paid, besides two guineas a year, twenty guineas when the subscription was opened, had a substantial surplus, of which a part is from time to time applied to the better completion of the whole. Notwithstanding this the shares in the old society have not fallen below 30 guineas. Besides newspapers and journals in all languages, which are kept by both literary societies, the works of the best authors in the sciences and fine arts are to be found in the libraries, and besides that, what one does not always find in large libraries, a crowd of readers.

The town has been adorned in recent years with several new and fine buildings, and they are now engaged in laying out whole streets and market places. Outside the town I saw some beautiful country houses, which for the most part had been built by business people of Liverpool.

A canal, which begins at Leeds in Yorkshire, and runs through a stretch of 12 or 13 Swedish miles in Lancashire in several loops terminates near the harbour in a great basin, the water level in which stands at least 13 yards higher than the streets below. The shores of this basin consist of large flat spaces, where coal and other goods are unloaded. Various smaller canals are linked to this one, and through the navigable rivers between Leeds and the Humber it opens to some extent a connection between the two seas. On another side of the town and a few English miles from it, the Bridgewater canal and the Grand Trunk, as well as two smaller ones, join the river Mersey, which is navigable up to Liverpool, and whose final junction with the sea is formed by the harbour and the inlet to the town itself. The situation of the town is therefore one of the most favourable for inland and foreign trade that can be imagined, and when one adds to that the industry, the thrift, and the already circulating capital of the inhabitants, it is easy to guess what has so far happened in business, and what may yet happen in future.

After a few days I travelled from Liverpool, where I parted from my Scottish travelling companion, who crossed to Ireland by the packet boat, to Manchester in company with Mr Bourne. This town, which in respect of population and manufactures has long since been one of the most important in England, has extended extraordinarily, especially in the last fifteen years, through its cotton manufactures. The number of its inhabitants is calculated at 70,000 to 80,000, who for the most part are engaged in this work. Several circumstances have united here to favour this branch of industry, among which the general use of the fine, white and light cotton fabric, which has almost supplanted the silk throughout Europe, may deserve the first place. Next to this comes the invention of the spinning machines, which first became common in Manchester, and are not only there brought to the greatest perfection, but also housed with an outward magnificence which is other-

wise not so common in the English factories.[29] As proof of
this a spinning mill may serve, where the building itself is
of brick, and in a good style, also the inside, which is otherwise normally of wood, is made either of dressed stone or
iron, to say nothing of some others in and outside the town,
whose fine installations and buildings enrich and adorn
the same. Almost all these spinning machines are driven
by steam engines, and in order to carry away the coal-
smoke, which could during finishing and packing of the
goods take away from them something of the dazzling whiteness given to them by artificial bleaching, the chimneys
at most of the mills are taken up high above the roofs,
and in some places arrangements are made to burn up
the smoke during the heating. With such a large demand
for coal, it is no small advantage to the town that even at
the present high prices it can have it about 50 per cent
cheaper than the coal cost a little over forty years ago,
before the Duke of Bridgewater's canal was finished, from
whose coalmines practically the whole of Manchester is
now supplied. The simplicity of transport on this canal to
Liverpool and several other canals in the country; the nearness of such a large commercial town, where for useful
undertakings there is never a lack of capitalists who make
important loans to the manufacturers or take their goods
on speculation, if the price falls too low; the ability, through
extensive and well-thought-out establishments, to accom-
modate themselves to the moods of fashion, instantly to
recover many times on one article, what has been lost on
another—all this, which generally contributes much to the
prosperity of the English factories, united with the local
circumstances mentioned above, gives this town an ascend-
ancy in manufacturing which must endure as long as the
customs and habits in Europe undergo no total change.
For even if one assumes the possibility of a complete lack
of sales, on account of war, financial upsets, etc, which is

174

predicted for England by many, what has been and will be the consequences thereof? That the manufacturer, in hopes of a better future, continues his work to the extreme, that the capitalist, as soon as the goods have fallen to a certain price, begins to buy on speculation, and that the latter, to avoid a greater loss, will likewise be obliged to sell below that price. From this it would necessarily seem to follow that the factories would stand still and some workers would be ruined: but before this came to pass, such a great quantity of goods, and at such low prices, would already have been spread throughout the whole world, that no incitements, no tariff regulations or prohibitions could prevent the further distribution of them. An extensive use, especially of wares of luxury and comfort, soon becomes a necessity, and thereafter there is no further question of price. The price of the goods goes up once more, the business man seeks to profit, as much as he can, the stopped factories are brought into operation, perhaps with more advantage than ever, partly due to the fallen prices of raw material, which always follows the dropping prices of the finished goods, partly because some factories are sold at half their value in the worst period, and thus come into the hands of well-to-do people, who, satisfied with a moderate profit, finally, and if business again begins to falter, reduce the prices, so that no country can compete with England, except through artificial and often disadvantageous regulations.

It could perhaps be objected that on such a faltering a great number of skilled workers would leave the country; however, the English constitution places important obstructions in the way of such an emigration, and those who nevertheless emigrated would certainly, upon the first sign of better times, be driven by homesickness to return to their fatherland; for the latter sickness affects the English perhaps more strongly than any other nation. Besides that, the arrangement of a factory on the English methods demands the employment of workers for diverse details, and an overseer who knows the whole thing from the ground up, to say nothing of the fact that a country which is now in possession of the trade of the world, must necessarily obtain most raw materials at a better price than other countries.

What I have now said about the preparation of cotton goods, and especially about the factories in Manchester, also holds indisputably for many other preparations and manufactures in England, and one can perhaps take it as certain that all competition in respect of manufactures is fruitless in two cases: that is, if the rival cannot almost alone dispose of the raw material without limitations, or if the manufacturing prices depend upon arrangements of such an extent that the capitalists of the country, upon lack of sales arising, either do not dare to offer the necessary loans, or cannot afford them. For this reason I have only been able to regard the cotton factories, the cutlery works, etc, of various countries, merely as innocent patriotic amusements, which, even though they are directly supported and encouraged by the government, can under such circumstances only train a few skilled workers, and only provide the country with certain articles when the demand arises. On the other hand every country has some factories, which are not dependent on the circumstances touched on above; which are, so to speak, natural to the country, among which can be numbered, by way of example, the manufacture of bar iron in Sweden, and the Swedish linen weaving industry in Norrland and part of West Gotland, for these must always, on account of the excellent quality of the goods or the possibility of a low price, be able at any time to compete with foreign manufactures of the same kind, even in the export trade.

During my stay in Manchester I made a tour to Worsley,

rather more than a Swedish mile from the town, from which a passenger boat, drawn by horses in the Dutch fashion, departs every day on the Bridgewater canal. The district, through which a part of this canal runs, is mostly low-lying and consists of flat meadows, until one comes to a place called Barton, where the canal crosses over the navigable River Irwell on an aqueduct 100 fathoms long and 40 feet high. Below the aqueduct is a road with a special bridge over the river, so that in passing here one sees road vehicles and boats several yards below. Between Barton and Worsley the countryside is less level, and the canal is walled in or embanked in several places. At Worsley the subterranean canal, 2,000 to 3,000 Swedish ells long begins, which is taken to the coalmines, where it divides into two branches on the surface, and is partially blasted through rock, partially walled. The coal is taken in waggons from the various working places in the mines, and tipped into boats of from 7 to 8 tons loading. Several of these boats, coupled together, are then taken to Worsley by men or horses through the underground canal, from where transport proceeds mostly to Manchester in larger boats.

This canal, in the building of which so many natural obstacles had to be overcome, is not merely remarkable for the benefits which the manufacturers of Manchester draw from it, but also on account of the boldness of the undertaking, the speed with which it was carried out, and its decisive influence on imitators. In the years 1758 and 1759, when the recently deceased Duke of Bridgewater obtained the first Acts of Parliament for the building of this canal, only a few small rivers had been made navigable by means of locks, but no work of this kind had been undertaken on the great plan of a horizontal channel of water over valleys and rivers and through mountains, to avoid the obstruction and expense of locks, and thereby to economise the water supply, fairly small in many parts of England. Scarcely had the Duke received permission, than he had already taken up the work at all points, and obtained possession, partly through purchase, partly through leasing, of the land through which the canal was to run. At the Duke's expense a great number of boats were built, before the water was even in the canal, because he alone wanted to draw the profits of the carrying trade. In two years the work was near to completion, but the fairly large fortune of the Duke was already exhausted, and his credit, on account of the enormous sums which he was seen to be expending on an undertaking which in the general opinion was so uncertain, was so weakened, that he could scarcely collect £1,000 with great exertion. It is said that at that time he limited his household for a little while to one servant and a pair of horses, but, as zealous as ever for the completion of his plan, and supported by some well-off friends, he was not long in this state of embarrassment. When the Duke died a few years ago, his annual income from the canal, the coalmines, and some other properties, besides the shares, was estimated at £120,000 sterling.

As proof of how this undertaking has encouraged similar ones, I may remark, that in the two years 1791 and 1792 over £5,300,000 sterling has been subscribed for canal works. In the same time, 36 Acts of Parliament were drafted for quite new undertakings of the kind, and counting in the older paid-off canal constructions and river clearances, 47. The many canals previously mentioned, like almost all those which are shown on Smith's Map of Inland Navigation, have a later origin than that of Bridgewater. Most of them are merely for boats of 8 to 20 tons loading, and so far as I know, none of them takes such large vessels as the canal at Trollhätta in Sweden.[30]

At Worsley there are some limekilns, a large furnace of iron plates, for converting coal into coke, and some nail forges, as well as several small installations which all belong to the owner of the canal.

The limekilns are 14 yards high and very broad, in the form of inverted cones. The burning is usually done with coal and chalk put in in layers, as in a blast furnace. When the lime is ready, it is hooked out at the bottom, and a fresh charge is put in at the top. Usually more than 100 Swedish tons of quicklime pass through such a furnace in 24 hours, which, broken up small or ground, is sold on the spot for one Swedish thaler per ton. The grinding is done with stones running vertically, and sometimes, when the lime is to be used for mortar, the requisite quantity of sand is mixed with it.

On returning to Manchester, I made, in company with Mr Bourne, another excursion of 5 or 6 Swedish quarter-miles to Rochdale, a little town on the way to Leeds, in order to see a canal construction which was being carried out there, and to be present at a meeting of the share-holders. The canal, which was already navigable, was now supposed to be continued through hilly and uneven country, for a few English miles. In the execution of this work several hindrances had occurred, partly because of the locality, partly because of the quarrelsome company, which now gave rise to such violent dissensions at the meeting, that the entire project could have been abandoned, if the share-holders had not been bound by an Act of Parliament to have the canal finished in a certain time. Meanwhile, considerable arrangements seem already to have been made here for the laying of railways, for facilitating transport and with the provision of hewn sandstone and chalk, which were both cut from the canal mentioned. Between Liverpool and Manchester, just as around the latter town, the country is densely built up and intensively cultivated.

The fear of inconveniencing myself, in consequence of the general suspicion of all foreigners now that war had broken out, induced me to set off immediately for London, otherwise I would have spent a longer time in these parts. I had been given some good addresses at some of the Derbyshire ironworks which I would have visited had I been able to stay but I decided that I ought not to be deterred from setting off immediately. I therefore took a so-called 'Opposition Coach'* direct to Derby, through several handsome, newly built towns, and a beautiful countryside alternating between flat, cultivated plains and hills and valleys. I got no more than a glimpse of these places, however, because I had allowed no more than $6\frac{1}{2}$ hours to cover nearly 8 Swedish miles.

At Derby I took a seat in the mail coach for London. Travelling so fast, however, one could take in no more for any part of the whole stretch of nearly 20 Swedish miles beyond noticing that it was extremely rich and attractive.

After some weeks' stay in London, I returned at the end of October on an English packet boat to the fatherland, when I immediately decided to publish a part of the notes I had made during my journey even with the many imperfections inevitable in work done so hastily and which an inexperienced author could not avoid.

*This coach, which takes four to six passengers and is drawn by two or three horses, is called an 'Opposition-Coach' because it sets out to compete with other coaches in terms both of speed and price. I came across many of these during my travels in England; but this kind of cut-throat competition seldom continues for long, because the owners of the other coaches are quickly ruined or are forced to give up for fear of bankruptcy.

Notes

By J. G. L. Blumhof

1. The Aliens Office is the place where the passports of all who are travelling out of England are issued, and those of persons arriving are examined. Aliens Offices of this kind which report to the head office in London are in almost all ports.

2. Mr Dryander has published a systematic catalogue of Mr Banks' [Sir Joseph Banks] library, of which I will here indicate only the title which contains mineralogy—Jonas Dryander, *Catalogus bibliothecae historico-naturalis Josephi Banks, Baroneti* (5 vols, London, 1798-1800).

3. In this connection, see *Neue Theorie des Strassenbaues, und über den Gebrauch der Eisenbahnen zu leichter Fortschaffung grosser Lasten* (Leipzig, 1801); 'Etwas über eiserne Fahrgleisen-Wege', in *Reichs-Anzeiger*, 1803, p327; *Blätter für Polizei und Kultur für 1801 bis 1803* (Tübingen, 1801-3), p1016. Tracks of this kind are said already to have been laid in Germany at Hattingen in the County of Mark. There are descriptions and improvements of these ways in the *Repertory of Arts, etc.*, III (1803), p15, and in the *Annales des Arts et Manufactures*, XIV, p312, and elsewhere.

4. This disadvantage is a principal reason why one still encounters so few steam engines in Germany. If we had such rich and extensive coal seams as the English, we should also gladly follow in their footsteps, but the operation of steam engines with charcoal is not profitable, and very few districts of Germany (if Silesia is included) have coal deposits, and these have indeed actually installed such engines, according to the extent of their productivity. That one must be very cautious in installing such an engine, which demands so much fuel, I learnt through an example at a certain brown coal works, where a steam engine set up for water pumping required as much coal, if not more, as was obtained from the mine. To the best of my knowledge, under these circumstances the engine had to be closed down.

5. See Thomas P. Smith, 'Note sur la fabrication du fer et de l'acier avec la honille d'après les procédés de M. William Reynolds, etc. Communiquée au Conseil des Mines, *Journal des Mines*, XIII (An 13), 52-60. In Germany this English iron refining process has already been made known in the year 1805 by a treatise by Herr von Bonnard, the travelling companion of our author. K. E. F. von Moll published an extract in *Ephemeriden der Berg und Hüttenkunde*, I, 383-404. We still, however, await Svedenstierna's fuller description. Because, however, the journal of von Moll may be in the hands of

N

most readers of this work, it is perhaps easier to refer to that and
leave it to the reader to make his own comparison.

6. In this calculation of coal and ore deposits, one must not imagine
the seams as extending over such an area; but as lying one above the
other in a narrow confine, the cubic capacity of which is equal to an
area of 2,000 acres and a certain depth.

7. Compare the description of a tour made from Hamburg to and
through England in summer 1799, by P. A. Nemnich, *Beschreibung
einer im Sommer 1799 von Hamburg nach und durch England
geschehenen Reise* (Tübingen, 1800), p337.

8. See *Account of the Qualities and Uses of Coal Tar and Coal Varnish.
With certificates from Ship-masters and others* (London, 1785); and
Johann Beckman, *Physikalisch-Ökonomische Bibliothek* (Göttingen,
1770), Vol 16, p225.

9. J. A. Hildt, *Handlungs Zeitung* (1790), p33, gives the length of the
bridge as 100 feet, the width as 24 feet, and the total weight as
11,000 cwt.

10. Information about this iron bridge near Coalbrookdale can also be
found in several publications. I will indicate a few of them here:
'Lettre de Mr Prevost-Dacier sur le pont de fer de Coalbrookdale',
in Rozier's *Observations et Mémoires sur la physique, etc.*, Vol 35
(1789), pp16-19 (German translation in the *Bergmannische Journal,*
II (1790), pp570-76); 'On the iron bridge at Coalbrookdale in England', in Hildt's *Handlungs Zeitung* (1790), p33. On iron bridges in
general, see Richard Warner, *A Tour through the Northern Coun-
ties of England and the Borders of Scotland* (Bath, 1802), Vol II,
p197; 'De Montpetit sur la Théorie des Ponts de fer d'une seule et
grande arc de trois à cinq cents pieds d'ouverture', in Rozier's
Journal de Physique, Vol 32; 'Specification of the patent granted to
Mr. John Nash . . .', *Repertory of Arts and Manufactures*, VI
1797), 361-8. The iron bridge built at Laasan in Silesia in 1796 at
the expense of the Graf von Burghaus probably also deserves a mention here. The weight of this bridge in cast- and wrought-iron
amounted to 946 cwt 181½ lb. The cost of the entire bridge including
labour, manufacturing, and transport charges was 6,711 Reichsthaler.
The greatest width of the arch is 40 feet, the height 9 feet and the
breadth of the bridge 18 feet. See Hildt's *Handlungs Zeitung* (1797),
p38, and *Schlesische Provinzialblätter*, (October, 1796), p368. An
accurate illustration of this bridge, which is the first of the kind in
Germany, is to be found in *Abbildung der Eisernen Waaren, welche
auf den Konigl. Preuss. Eisenwerken zu Malapane, Gleiwitz und
Greuzburg in Schlesien gegossen werden* (Leipzig), and in the *Samm-
lung nützl. Aufsätze und Nachrichten, die Baukunst Betreff,* 1 (1797),
p167. To commemorate the building of this bridge a copper medal,
which I possess myself, has been struck. On one side is the perspective
view of the bridge, over the centre of which hovers an eagle, with the
arms of the builder. Below reads: SPANNUNG 40 FUSS. HOEHE—
9. BREITE—18. ERRICHTET 1796. Around the edge: ZUM AN-
DENKEN DER ERSTEN EISERNEN BRUECKE IN SCHLESIEN.

On the reverse: AUF KOSTEN DES HERRN REICHSGRAFEN NICLAS AUGUST VON BURGHAUS AUF LAASAN—GEBOREN 14 Maertz 1750. Around the edge: HERRN VON LAASAN PETRE-WITZ SARAU BEATENWALD UND NEUDORF. The medal is about the size of a Brabant half-thaler, only much thicker. A second iron bridge, likewise cast in a Silesian iron foundry, is erected over the Kupfergraben in Berlin. The castings for it weigh 1,288 cwt and cost, including the screws, etc, delivered to Breslau, 4,720 Reichsthaler. It is also illustrated in the first booklet of the above-mentioned collection of engravings of Silesian castings.

11. See Sven Rinman, *Allgemeines Berkverks-lexicon* (trans. J. G. L. Blumhof, Leipzig, 1808), Part 2, p773.

12. Concerning this and several other canals in England, see J. L. Hogreve, *Beschreibung der in England seit 1759 angelegten, und jetzt grössentheils vollendeten schiffbaren Kanäle* (Hannover, 1780).

13. See J. H. M. von Poppe, *Encyclopädie des gesammten Maschinenwesens* (Leipzig, 1820-27), Vol 2, p85.

14. 'Résultats d'expériences sur les différents états du fer, par le Cit. Clouet', in the *Journal des Mines*, An 7 [1799], pp3-12; Guyton, 'Rapport sur les résultats des expériences du Cit. Clouet sur les différent états du fer, et pour la conversion du fer en acier fondu', *Annales de Chemie*, Vol 28, pp19-39; *Journal des Mines*, An 6, No 45, p703 (German translation in Crell's *Chemische Annalen* (1800, Pt. 2), pp55-65). A report of the attempts of Clouet and the Englishman Mushet to make steel is to be found in O'Reilly's *Annales des Arts et Manufactures*, Vol IV, p25. And see Mushet on the conversion of bar iron or good iron ore into cast steel, as well as an appendix by Herr Bergrat von Crell, in the latter's *Chemische Annalen* (1800, pt. 2), p50. The Mushet process for preparing all kinds of steel is also described in the same issue, p218 ff.

15. B. F. J. von Hermann, *Ueber die Frage, worin besteht der Unterschied zwischen Roheisen und geschmeidigern Eisen aus Frischheerden?* (Leipzig, 1799).

16. *Mémoire sur l'acier, dans lequel on traite des différentes qualités de ce metal, de la forge: du bon emploi et de la trempe; ouvrage couronné par le Société des arts de Genève* (1779). See my systematic bibliography of iron—J. G. L. Blumhof, *Biblioteca Ferri* (Brunswick, 1803).

17. Old Sabel or Sable, because the Siberian ironworks at Tagil so names its iron to distinguish it from the New Sable, which is made at the ironworks at Kushva, and ranks after the first-named in quality. However, all Siberian-Russian iron is stamped with a sable. See J. E. Norberg, *Ueber die Produktion des Roheisens in Russland* (Trans. from Swedish by J. G. L. Blumhof, Freyberg, 1805), p16.

18. Six Hull chaldrons are equal to eight London ones, and a chaldron in London amounts to 9¾ tons in Swedish measure.

19. This kind of process has much similarity to the method of coal-tar

distillation used at Sulzbach in the county of Saarbrück. More detailed information about it is to be found in Johann Beckmann, *Anleitung zur Technologie oder zur Kenntnis der Handwerke, Fabriken und Manufacturen* (Göttingen, 1777). (5th ed Göttingen, 1802), p471; and the same author's *Beyträge zur Oekonomie, Technologie, Polizey und Cameralwissenschaft* (Göttingen, 1779-91), Vol 8, p104.

20. Barilla is a fused mass from the burnt salt wort (*Salicornia*) and soda wort (*Salsola*, especially *S. sativa L.*), which grow plentifully in Spain around Murcia and Alicante. They are burnt in bushels either in limekilns or in ditches provided with an iron grate. When the plant is burning it flows out in the pit or below the grate, and is found upon cooling as a stone-hard, grey, and porous mass, which is called barilla and is used in glass-making and soap-boiling. See G. A. Suckow, *Anfangsgründe der theoretischen und angewandten Botanik* (Leipzig, 1786), Vol 2, p235; and Strelin's *Realwörterbuch für Kameralisten und Oekonomen*, Vol 2, p65.

21. See 'Sur la construction des ponts de fer, avec la description d'un pont de 236 pieds d'ouverture, construit à Wearmouth en Angleterre', *Annales des Arts et Manufactures*, II, 166-173.

22. The gathering of kelp constitutes a principal means of livelihood of people living near the coast there and in other parts of Europe, so that the Highland Society in Scotland has offered a prize on this account. The award-winning prize essay is in *Repertory of Arts and Manufactures*, XII (1800), p243. There are several essays on this subject, translated from the English, in Rafn's *Nyr Bibliothek for Physik, Medicin og Oekonomie* (Copenhagen), Vol. I. The London Economic Society had already, in 1768, demanded kelp of the same quality as the Spanish barilla, and also offered a prize for it. See Beckman's *Physikalisch-Ökonomische Bibliothek* (Göttingen, 1770), Vol 3, p548. In the Scilly Isles kelp is burnt from *Fucus vesiculosus*, and in some Hebridean islands this salt is obtained from ferns. See William Borlase, *Observations on the Ancient and Present State of the Islands of Scilly . . .* (Oxford, 1756); Thomas Pennant, *A Tour in Scotland and Voyage to the Hebrides* (2 pts Chester & London, 1774-76); William Hamilton, *Letters concerning the Northern Coast of the County of Antrim* (Dublin, 1786; trans. L. Crell, *Briefe über die nördliche Küste der Grafschaft Antrim*, Leipzig, 1787).

23. This has now appeared—Robert Jameson, *An Outline of the Mineralogy of the Shetland Islands and of the Island of Arran* (Edinburgh, 1798; German translation by H. W. Meuder, Leipzig, 1802).

24. For German readers the following have so far been published: J. F. Westrumb, *Praktische Bemerkungen und Vorschläge für Branntweinbrenner* (Hannover, 1793); *Neues Magazin der Künste und Wissenschaften für Gelehrte, Kunstler, Oekonomen, etc*, Vol 1 (Leipzig, 1803); C. C. A. Neuenhahn, *Die Branntweinbrennerei nach Theoretischen und praktischen Grundsätzen* (Leipzig, 1801-4), Vol 2, where the Scottish equipment, so far as it is now known, which is

imperfectly, has been described. These may be difficult for German distillers to adapt, because according to Herr Westrumb, op cit p99, they require experienced and judicious proprietors, and, moreover, are based upon the output of spirit usual in Scotland. It would have been very helpful if Herr Westrumb had described the Scottish distilling installations by means of a good drawing. See also Johann Beckman, *Physikalisch-Ökonomische Bibliothek* (Göttingen, 1770), Vol 22.

25. Anyone who desires information about this ironworks, as it was in the year 1765, will find detailed information about it in Gabriel Jars, *Voyages Métallurgiques* (3 vols, Lyon & Paris, 1774-81), German translation by C. A. Gerhard, 4 vols Berlin, 1775-85) (see Vol 2, p442). More recent information is in J. J. Ferber, *Neue Beyträge zur Mineralgeschichte verschiedener Länder* (Miebau, 1778), Vol I, p453; William Nimmo, *A General History of Stirlingshire . . . with the natural history of the shire* (Edinburgh, 1777); Thomas Pennant, *A Tour in Scotland* (Chester, 1771).

26. A good deal of information about lifeboats for shipwrecked seafarers is to be found in J. H. M. Poppe, *Allgemeine Rettungsbuch* (Hannover, 1805) which received the prize offered by Count von Berchtold of Vienna. The prize essay of the Englishman, Fothergill, on the means of rescue at sea (Anthony Fothergill, *An Essay on the Preservation of Shipwrecked Mariners* (London, 1799) has been interwoven into this work, for which every humanitarian will be grateful to the author and to the unfortunately recently deceased prizegiver. Fothergill received the prize offered by the Royal Humane Society in London in 1800, and Count von Berchtold translated the essay, and had it printed, enriched with comments and additions.

27. In some districts of the Duchy of Westphalia and the adjoining Waldeck and Berleburg, etc, some kinds of thin cakes of oatmeal and potatoes are cooked in a similar fashion on the ordinary living-room stoves, which are there called 'Giesecken', also 'Ofenkuchen' and 'Ofenplatz'. This baking is done on the upper plate of the strongly heated stove, and not seldom gives rise to an almost unbearable vapour in the anyway low peasant living-rooms, to say nothing of the fact that these seldom properly cooked pastries must be very unhealthy for weak stomachs.

28. All classes of people are engaged in this infamous trade in Liverpool: clergymen, lawyers, craftsmen, and so-called humanitarians. Admittedly the town has made extraordinary sums from it, and P. A. Nemnich, *Beschreibung einer in Sommer 1799 von Hamburg nach und durch England geschehenen Reise* (Tübingen, 1800), p337, relates that the profit from 303,737 slaves which were handled by Liverpool ships in a period of ten years, amounted to a sum of £15,186,850. Otherwise, what Mr Svedenstierna relates about the treatment of the slaves on the English slave ships does the nation credit, and it is to be hoped that this detestable traffic in human beings will soon disappear through the efforts of Wilberforce, Lord Grenville, and several English humanitarians. However, if anyone wants to inform himself

more closely about this trade and the cruelties and atrocities which have been and are being committed in the treatment of the negroes in the colonies, especially the French ones, I refer him to the following: Anthony Benezet, *Some Historical account of Guinea* (Philadelphia, 1771); J. B. C. T. Aublet, *Histoire des Plantes de la Guiane Françoise* (London & Paris, 1775); Weuves, le jeune, *Réflexions historiques et politiques sur le commerce de France avec ses colonies de l'Amérique* (Geneva & Paris, 1780) (particularly important for a knowledge of the French slave trade); *Essai sur l'Histoire Naturelle de l'Isle de Saint-Domingue* (Paris, 1776); *Le Guide du Commerce de l'Amérique, etc.* (2 vols, Avignon and Marseilles, 1777); O. C. Menzel, *Geographische und Topographische Beschreibung des Afrikanischen Vorgebürges der guten Hoffnung, etc.* (Glogau, 1785); *Affiches, Annonces et Avis divers, ou Journal général de France* (1784 and 1785); P. E. Isert, *Reise nach Guinea und den Caribäischen Inseln in Columbien, in Briefen an seine Freunde beschrieben* (Copenhagen, 1788); J. F. Ludwig (ed P. F. Binder), *Herrn J. F. L.'s neueste Nachrichten von Surinam* (Jena, 1789); John Matthews, *A Voyage to the River Sierra-Leone* (London, 1788); M.P.D.P., *Description de la Négritie* (Amsterdam, 1789) (see Johann Beckman, *Physikalisch-Ökonomische Bibliothek* (Göttingen, 1770) vol 16, p298): A. M. Rochon, *Voyage à Madagascar et eux Indes Orientales* (Paris, 1791); Hans West, *Bidrag til beskrivelse over Ste. Croix, med en kort udsigt over St. Thomas, St. Jean, Tortola, Spanishtown og Crabeneiland* (Copenhagen, 1793); Sir George L. Staunton, *An authentic account of an Embassy from the King of Great Britain to the Emperor of China* (2 vols London, 1797); B. A. Euphrasen. *Beskrifning öfver Svenska vestindiska ön St. Barthelemi, samt öarne St. Austache och St. Christopher* (Stockholm, 1795) (Translated into German by J. G. L. Blumhof, Göttingen, 1798).

There is also a remarkable essay on this subject in the February 1810 issue of von Archenholtz's *Minerva*, under the title: 'Gegenwärtiger zustand der Negersklaven im brittischen Westindien, besonders in den von Britten eroberten holländischen Kolonien, nebst einer Apologie des Neger-sklavenhandels'. ['The present condition of the negro slaves in the British West Indies, particularly in the Dutch colonies conquered by the British, together with an apology for the negro slave trade.'] From the English of Henry Bolinbroke. However, I only know this treatise from the newspaper advertisements for the *Minerva* issue.

29. The following works can be recommended to anyone who wishes further to inform himself about the rapid progress of the English spinning machines and their improvement: J. H. M. Poppe, *Geschichte der Technologie seit der Wiederherstellung der Wissenschaften bis an das Ende des achtzehnten Jahrhunderts* (Göttingen, 1796), Vol I, p274. Particularly comprehensive information about Manchester can be found in P. A. Nemnich, *Beschreibung einer in Sommer 1799 von Hamburg nach und durch England geschehenen Reise* (Tübingen, 1800). Richard Arkwright, originally a poor barber, received in 1775 a patent for the improvement of the spinning

machine, which, however, was withdrawn in 1785, because his right to the invention was not fully proved. However, he left a fortune of more than half a million thalers (*Journal für Fabrik, Handlung, und Mode* (1794), p196).

30. More exhaustive information about the layout of the canal of Bridgewater, and the undertakings connected with it can be found in the following works: Anon., *The History of Inland Navigation, particularly those of the Duke of Bridgewater in Lancashire and Cheshire* 2nd ed., London, 1769) of which Professor Beckman has published a complete extract in *Physikalisch-Ökonomische Bibliothek* (Göttingen, 1770), II, p1; Arthur Young, *A Six Months' Tour through the North of England* (London, 1770), Vol III, pp251, 310; J. L. Hogreve, *Beschreibung der in England seit 1759 angelegten, und jetzt grössentheils vollendeten schiffbaren Kanäle* (Hannover, 1780).

Index